Record of a Sol

John Wesley Bone

Record of a Soldier in the Late War

The Confederate Memoir of
John Wesley Bone

Edited by

Julianne Mehegan

David Mehegan

CHINQUAPIN PUBLISHERS

On the cover: Lyrics of a Confederate soldier's song, written from memory by John Wesley Bone at age 85. The song is usually titled "The Rebel Soldier," with the word "rebel" throughout, but JWB uses the word "Southern."

Published by Chinquapin Publishers
Hingham, Massachusetts
www.confederatememoir.com

Copyeditor: Elizabeth Uhrig
Cover and interior design, typesetting: Janis Owens

ISBN: 978-0-692-21049-9

LIBRARY OF CONGRESS CONTROL NUMBER: 2014939478

PRINTED IN THE UNITED STATES OF AMERICA

For the Bone family, past, present, and future.

Contents

Editors' Preface

"A Place on the Record"

John Wesley Bone's *Record of a Soldier in the Late War* is the memoir of a Southern youth in the American Civil War. But it is much more than that; it is also the story of every good-hearted, naive country boy who goes off to war with no conception of what awaits him.

John Wesley Bone, age eighteen, enlisted in the 30th Regiment of North Carolina Volunteers on September 10, 1861. He surrendered with the Army of Northern Virginia at Appomattox Court House on April 9, 1865, age twenty-three. During those three and a half years, he fought in several of the greatest battles of the war. Despite many close brushes with death, he eluded long odds and lived to write this story forty years later, while confined to his sickbed. That illness, too, he survived, to live another thirty-two years, into his nineties.

History is not confined to the details of events that are fully provable, as mathematical propositions are provable. It is also about the telling and the tellers. Thousands of books have been written about those epic events and passionate years, many with sweeping perspectives. But like that of every individual soldier, John Wesley Bone's part was local, limited, and unique. He was aware of his limits. Nevertheless, in early old age he became concerned that his personal memories have "a place on the record." That desire, which drove him "in my free hours from pain" to lie and write, produced this gift to us and generations to come.

No soldier on either side of this conflict could have been more common than John Wesley Bone. He won no decorations, received no official commendations, and is unmentioned in official histories. He enlisted as a private and surrendered as a private. Although his testimony does not redirect the broad understanding of historians, still he has few peers in the range and variety of his witness of large things and small. He had virtually every kind of experience that a Civil War soldier could have, save capture and death. He writes of suicidal charges against massed cannon and musket fire, of the sorrow of burial duty, of eating and drinking and waiting, of sickness and endless marching and camping, of worn-out shoes and bleeding feet, of loneliness and the longing for a comforting feminine touch. We do not learn much about the big picture of battles; often it is not clear where John Wesley is in them or what exactly is happening. But his descriptions of actions have directness and clarity. For drama and suspense, the incredible story of his escape from death at the Battle of Spotsylvania Court House has few equals.

His encounters with disease were as fearsome and dangerous as the battles. The consolations of religion and the continual preaching to the troops by chaplains are a constant theme and help to sustain him. Besides all this, John Wesley Bone's memory for detail gives us the call of the whip-poor-will in the night before battle, the blaring of bands, and the poignant last orders at Appomattox. Amid the grim chronicle of terror, slaughter, and misery there are flashes of humor and even one pretty good joke.

While memoirists on both sides often wrote in stirring terms of the great cause, John Wesley Bone does not. His account is devoid of politics. Governments and slavery are unmentioned. He served because to do otherwise, in his close-knit community and society, was unthinkable. He tells what he did, saw, felt, and thought over three and a half terrible years. Whether the leaders were right or wrong was for others to decide. His is a straightforward story of comradeship, duty, obedience, and endurance — as he puts it, "of going steadily forward, taking and bearing realities of a soldier in war."

THE FOREBEARS OF JOHN WESLEY BONE came to eastern North Carolina from Virginia in about 1780, acquiring land in the area around what is today Nash and Edgecombe counties.[1] John Wesley was the fifth generation of Bones in Nash County. His grandfather Nelson Bone was prosperous enough to buy and sell parcels of land, at about one dollar per acre, amassing a thousand acres by 1850.

The Bone family made their living as farmers, raising cotton and corn. In the early nineteenth century, cotton was the sole money crop. Corn was raised to feed livestock and to be ground into meal for cooking. Most of the farmwork was done by the family. It was traditional in the family to make brandy to supplement income. Nelson inherited a brandy still from his father, and his account records show that he sold brandy in pints and quarts. At the time of his death in 1866, one brandy still was sold for fifty dollars. Nelson and Mourning Bone had four sons: David, William, Calvin, and John, and one daughter, Rhoda. They in turn had eighteen children who lived into adulthood. David Bone paid his father one hundred dollars in 1840 for 162 acres of land. By 1848, his taxable land was 259 acres. According to the 1860 census, this real estate and other personal property was valued at $1,100.

David and Dinah Bone had four sons: John Wesley (b. 1842), Henry Austin (b. 1845), Josiah Nelson (b.1852), and Tinah Armile (b. 1854). Their house had one large room, twenty feet square, with a stairway to the attic, where the boys usually slept. The kitchen was detached from the house, as was common practice to limit the danger of fire. In a 1930 letter to the local newspaper, John Wesley wrote that he and his brothers "had all attended . . . the 'Old field School,' or 'Common School' it was called. By the side of the road or path stood a log building 14 x 18 with two doors and one window, a chimney and an open fireplace at one end. The scholars were seated around on split log benches. Our books were composed of an old Blue-Back Webster Speller, Smith's Arithmetic and Geography, and an English grammar. One teacher taught 30 to 40 scholars. Some of them walking from four to five miles to reach the school." The school term was three to four months a year.

From census data we learn that black people lived in the household of John Wesley's parents and grandparents. His grandfather Nelson Bone listed one slave in the 1820 census. John Wesley's mother (Dinah Poland Bone) experienced chronic headaches and illness. A woman slave, probably from her father's household, lived with the family to help with domestic tasks and the raising of the four boys. In the 1860 federal census, David and Dinah Bone's household included John Wesley (seventeen), Henry (thirteen), Josiah (nine), Tinah (four), and one female slave, Ferbra, age forty-nine years. She was affectionately called Aunt Ferbra.

John Wesley grew up with black people providing services for the family in a seemingly congenial relationship. His nephew Kenneth Bone recalled, "I heard Papa [Josiah Nelson Bone] say that he and Uncle Tinah [Tinah Armile Bone], as little boys, used to go out to the kitchen and sleep with Aunt Ferbra. They would sleep out there with her sometimes and they got up and get pickings while she was cooking breakfast." After the Civil War, Ferbra was free. She left the Bone household but continued to visit the family. As was common, Ferbra, as a slave, took the family's surname as her own. The 1880 federal census lists Ferbra Bone in the household of her sister, Mourning Ricks.

Many of John Wesley's relatives saw action in the Civil War. His brother Henry joined the Junior Reserve, moving up to the 30th Regiment N.C. Infantry when he turned eighteen. John Wesley's uncle John Bone was a private in the 10th Battalion N.C. Artillery. Hardy Bone, his cousin, was also in the 30th Regiment, enlisting the same day as John Wesley. He died of pneumonia at a Richmond hospital in 1862. John Thomas Bone, another cousin, was in the 43rd Regiment. His cousin Vincent Batchelor served in the 33rd Regiment and died at Winchester, Virginia, in 1862.

The regimental record shows that a large number of volunteers joined in Nashville on September 10, five months after the shelling of Fort Sumter, which might suggest some kind of enlistment event, perhaps advertised beforehand. It was a six-month enlistment. The volunteers were sent to Raleigh, the state capital, where John Wesley was assigned to the 30th Regiment. The regiment was transported by train to the coast at Wilmington, then to Southport, near Fort Caswell at the mouth of the Cape Fear River. Drilling and training began, as did the first of John Wesley's many illnesses. In March 1862, he and most of the regiment reenlisted for three years.

The following May, Union general George McClellan began the Peninsula Campaign with the intention of seizing Richmond, the Confederate capital. The N.C. 30th was rushed to Richmond and assigned to General Robert E. Lee's Army of Northern Virginia. Immediately the regiment participated in the disastrous assault on Union positions atop Malvern Hill. In August, John Wesley was stricken with illness and fell behind the army. He missed the Second Battle of Manassas on August 28–30, but while trying to catch up to the army, passed through the corpse-strewn battlefield and was shocked at the sight. The army had crossed the Potomac en route to the Battle of Antietam, September 17, but John Wesley and other barefoot stragglers were blocked by Confederate officers and sent west, between Harpers Ferry and

Winchester. In December he was sent back to his regiment in time for the December 11–15 Battle of Fredericksburg. The 30th Regiment was held in reserve and missed the worst of the fighting, then spent the winter on picket duty on the Rappahannock River.

In May 1863, John Wesley was part of Stonewall Jackson's famous flank march around the Union right at the Battle of Chancellorsville and the defeat of Union forces under General Joseph Hooker. On June 1, the army marched west and north, en route to Pennsylvania. On the way, John Wesley was stricken by another severe fever and hospitalized. He eventually improved enough to be furloughed home but had missed the Battle of Gettysburg. He rejoined his regiment in October. In December, the army was on the march again, but again John Wesley was stricken with illness. He was evacuated to the hospital in Charlottesville, where he spent the winter.[2]

Fully recovered by March 1864, John Wesley was ordered back to his regiment. In early May, the Wilderness Campaign began, with General Ulysses S. Grant driving south toward Lee's army. Lee rushed south to head off Grant's march toward Spotsylvania Court House, a crossroads within striking distance of Richmond. In the battle there on May 12, John Wesley was severely wounded in the chest. He lay between the lines for three days and most of a third night, finally crawling and staggering back to the new Confederate position.

In most wars, this would have been the end of a soldier's service. But in early October, John Wesley again rejoined his regiment, in the Shenandoah Valley, just in time for the Battle of Cedar Creek. In the middle of the Confederate rout, with Union forces in hot pursuit, he ran and stumbled alone through woods and across streams, eventually rejoining the scattered remains of the army.

That December, troops in the Shenandoah were loaded on frigid boxcars at Staunton, Virginia, and sent east to join Lee's army, dug in at Petersburg, south of Richmond. In April, the increasingly outflanked Confederate position became untenable. Pursued and harried on all sides, the shrunken Army of Northern Virginia plodded west. They marched and fought, day after day, until they reached Appomattox Court House. On April 9, Lee surrendered. After the surrender ceremony on April 12, John Wesley Bone and seventeen other North Carolinians started their last march, without arms or orders, one hundred fifty miles to their homes.

THE STORYTELLING MANNER IN *Record of a Soldier in the Late War* has a transparent plainness and simplicity. The writer announces at the start that he is not an educated man and lacks "perfect . . . language." The only literary work he mentions is the Bible, and that only a few times. Nevertheless, he is literate, spells well, and makes but few grammatical errors. His narration is vivid and clear except in the chaos of battle. In such scenes, his occasional cloudiness and errors add verisimilitude, since a crystal-clear account would make us suspect that postwar research and hundreds of retellings have smoothed away memory's jagged edges and odd details.

Many postwar memoirs of common soldiers make the war sound like an excellent adventure. Texan William A. Fletcher's 1908 memoir, *Rebel Private: Front and Rear,* combines picaresque yarn-spinning with a chilling gusto in killing. John Wesley Bone never celebrates death on either side. His shock and grief at the carnage of battle are manifest. Nor does he ever use the romantic words common in Civil War narratives, especially those by officers and educated men: *chivalry, gallantry, valor, glory.* In his postwar regimental history, Colonel Francis M. Parker, who commanded the 30th Regiment, writes of one battle, "On this field Colonel Sillers offered his young life on the altar of his country."[3] John Wesley

Bone writes, "Colonel Sillers was killed." His business is to tell what happened as best he remembers it, not to gild the story with hifalutin rhetoric.

His memoir, as well as all that we know about him otherwise, reveals a person of courage and character. He records his suffering without complaining about it. He does not hide his emotions: crushing despondency, fear of death, and "the low grounds of sorrow." He does not judge inept generals or the Confederate government's conduct of the war. Only once does he write reproachfully of an officer, for what seems to be paralysis in battle, and he almost never disparages a fellow soldier. Twice he digresses to recount the plight of women caught in the fighting. Unlike Parker, who writes, "Let us pray that we may annihilate the invading devils," John Wesley shows no rancor toward the enemy.[4] He even makes excuses for their sparse provision of food to the hungry Confederates after the surrender.

Among the central concerns of this memoir are Christian morals and the struggles of men in war to understand God's motives. Although John Wesley Bone says nothing about his or his family's church life before the war, it is clear from the beginning that he is imbued with Christian conviction. His faith seems firm throughout, yet at times he strives to make sense of God's will and has to push himself to accept the management of the "higher power."

Notwithstanding John Wesley Bone's simple and transparent manner, we are left with questions. Why does he almost never give the names of his fellow soldiers? With a single exception, only officers and the regimental chaplain are named. He seems at times to be one young man among thousands of nameless ghosts. How is it that the extraordinary violence he endured and participated in did not brutalize him, make him cold or bitter? Did he suffer from post-traumatic stress disorder — troubled by flashbacks or nightmares in later life? What were his true thoughts and feelings about the Confederate cause? It is difficult to imagine that he had none, even as a youth. To these questions we can answer only with speculations.

His devotion to duty was relentless. It was not so with all of his comrades. Nearly 24,000 North Carolina men deserted in the course of the war, including dozens from the 30th Regiment.[5] The thought of doing so must have entered John Wesley's mind, but to abandon his fellows was, evidently, impossible. Time and again, after dangerous illness and a nearly fatal wound, he got back on his feet and reported for duty — on one occasion near the end of the war, walking eighty miles to find his regiment. However we might in retrospect deplore his cause, we must say that in any fight, John Wesley Bone was the kind of person you would want on your side. He was *semper fideles.*

In long retrospect, the Civil War seems inevitable and fixed in our national memory. We enjoy visiting its battlefields and pondering stirring deeds and epic events. Those who survived could look back, perhaps, and find patriotic or religious meaning in it. But the story of John Wesley Bone reminds us that for those who have lived through war, "its glory is all moonshine," as General William T. Sherman famously said.[6] For them, it was a long, ugly nightmare of terror, sickness, butchery, exposure, near-starvation, and exhaustion. Indeed, John Wesley does not nearly detail its horror as he might have. To those hundreds of thousands who fought, the meaning of the war, and the bonds of comradeship it forged, was beyond the reach of ordinary words. John Wesley spoke for millions of common soldiers on both sides when he wrote of war's end, "We cannot express our feelings nor can others realize them at this point. . . . We had known for four years that military discipline was connected with go and come at its command and take what it gave us to eat and wear. . . . As we told each other good-bye, you could hear all around these words: Remember how we laid and bled together on the battlefield, or side by side in the hospital, or through the cold winter in some prison. Many of us have not seen or heard from each other since that morning."

SOME CIVIL WAR HISTORIANS have questioned the reliability of long-delayed memoirs such as *Record of a Soldier in the Late War* as evidence of the common man's experience, especially of his views and feelings about the war as it was going on.[7] Indeed, we *should* keep in mind that *Record of a Soldier in the Late War* is not the fresh testimony of a twenty-three-year-old, but that of a sixty-two-year-old whose narration follows four decades of life experience and reflection. We have no way of knowing what tone and attitudes he might have shown had he kept a diary or written wartime letters (if he wrote letters home, none survives). However, fundamental temperament ordinarily does not change much, even in forty years. Given the kind of person he was, John Wesley Bone likely *was* free of rancor at the end of the war. As for the facts of his story, there is no reason to doubt that he does his best to tell the truth as he remembers it. He is not writing a picaresque entertainment for money. While granting the occasional distortions of memory, we can accept that the events of the war were, in his word, "printed" on his mind. At the beginning and the end of the memoir, he assures us that although not everything that happened is here, everything that is here happened.

BECAUSE IT IS SOMETIMES DIFFICULT to figure out what *is* happening in *Record of a Soldier in the Late War,* as well as where and even when it happens, footnotes clarify and supplement the narrative.[8] The notes also relate John Wesley Bone's experience to the larger historical context. They pay special attention to an aspect of John Wesley Bone's war in which reenactors and battle buffs have little interest, but which was almost universal to the wartime experience: sickness, disease, evacuations, nursing, hospitals, and medical care generally. In some places where he uses the word *we,* John Wesley is describing events involving his regiment or the army that he did not witness directly. A few anecdotes appear to be based on hearsay. Apart from these, however, his descriptions of where he went and what he did are clear and largely accurate according to what is known from other accounts.

The memoir is followed by an appendix: the text of John Wesley Bone's written account, published in his hometown newspaper, of his return for the first time to Spotsylvania and other battlefields in 1925, at age eighty-four. So far as is known, these written words — with a poignant ending — are his last about the war. A few details of memory differ from the 1904 memoir, but his gentle personality, and his sense of awe in the face of the "Higher Power's" motives and expectations of him, shine through as they did twenty years earlier.

About the Text

Although the handwritten manuscript of *Record of a Soldier in the Late War* is lost, we believe this edition is faithful to the original. A typed copy, crudely stapled with an oilcloth cover, was the only transcript known to exist. It was kept in a particular chest drawer in the Bone family home but rarely looked at. It was always said by John Wesley's granddaughters that the memoir had been typewritten by a family friend, Ross Vaughan. They never remembered seeing a handwritten copy. In the 1970s, when copy machines became available, a photocopy was made and printed on standard office paper. Over the years several family members made copies, but as far as we knew the memoir was known only to the family. The family learned later that a copy of the Bone memoir was part of a collection of Confederate veteran remembrances at the North Carolina archives. These remembrances were collected by the United Daughters of the Confederacy in 1920.

As we began research for this project, Julianne visited the State Archives of North Carolina in Raleigh to examine the memoir in the collection. She saw that the typeface and spacing of the version there was different from the version the family had. Conversations with

other family members and Vaughan's daughter led to the discovery
that the family's bound copy had been typed in 1938. Thus we knew
that the handwritten memoir was transcribed twice, in 1920 by
someone who typed it for the UDC and again in 1938, when John
Wesley's grandson Walter Bone asked Vaughan to type it.

For this edition, the 1920 version was compared word for word
with the 1938 version. They proved to be almost identical. In a few
cases, one version supplies a small number of words dropped or
garbled by the transcriber of the other. Such variants have been
reconciled in this edition. Since there were so few, we made a case-
by-case choice as to which version to use. Had only one version
survived, the accuracy or completeness of the transcription could
not be known. The survival of separate, almost identical versions,
made eighteen years apart by different hands, gives a kind of bin-
ocular view of the lost original — strong evidence, we believe, that
this edition reproduces the words that John Wesley Bone wrote by
hand. Moreover, the clarity of his penmanship gives us added confidence in the accuracy of the typescripts and this edition. Several
samples of his handwriting exist. It was neat and legible as late as
1928, when he was eighty-six.

The typewritten text runs on without section breaks. To make
the narrative more manageable to the reader, we have broken
it into nine titled sections, corresponding with time periods or
events. Some extremely long paragraphs have been divided. In a
few instances, simple errors of grammar and punctuation, as well as
misspellings, have been silently corrected for clarity (for example:
parole replaces *payroll, memorable* replaces *memorial, Mechanicsville*
replaces *Maconsville*). Otherwise, the words are preserved as John
Wesley Bone wrote them.

Notes

1 For the history of the Bone family, including that of John Wesley Bone after the war, we are indebted to Frederick Holmes Cron, whose tireless work and careful compilation is recorded in *The Bone Family: Distant Voices as Heard from the Water's Edge* (Wyandotte, Okla.: The Gregath Publishing Company, 1999).

2 Such repeated attacks of life-threatening illnesses were typical. Of the at least 620,000 soldiers who died on both sides over the four years, two out of three were brought down by disease. Drew Gilpin Faust, *This Republic of Suffering: Death and the American Civil War* (New York: Alfred A. Knopf, 2008), 4. The 620,000 figure has been the standard total for more than a century, but a recent paper by historian David Hacker of Binghamton University raised the estimate by 20 percent, to 750,000. Guy Gugliotta, "New Estimate Raises Civil War Death Toll," *New York Times,* April 3, 2012, D1. Faust cites the higher figure in the 2012 Ric Burns film, *Death and the Civil War,* which is based on her book. *American Experience: Death and the Civil War,* PBS, September 18, 2012.

3 F. M. Parker, "Thirtieth Regiment," in *Histories of the Several Regiments and Battalions from North Carolina in the Great War 1861–'65,* Walter Clark, ed., vol. 2 (Raleigh, N.C.: E. M. Uzzell, 1901), 503.

4 For Parker's attitude toward the enemy, see Michael W. Taylor, *To Drive the Enemy from Southern Soil: The Letters of Colonel Francis Marion Parker and the History of the 30th Regiment North Carolina Troops* (Dayton, Ohio: Morningside House), 181.

5 Ella Lonn, *Desertion During the Civil War* (Lincoln: University of Nebraska Press, 1998; originally published 1928), 231.

6 Commonly attributed, apparently without a written record, to an address at the Michigan Military Academy, June 19, 1879.

7 See, for example, Aaron Sheehan-Dean, ed., *The View from the Ground: Experiences of Civil War Soldiers* (Lexington: University Press of Kentucky, 2007), 27.

8 For the movements and many other details of the 30th North Carolina Regiment, we relied greatly on Michael W. Taylor's 1998 book, *To Drive the Enemy from Southern Soil: The Letters of Colonel Francis Marion Parker and the History of the 30th Regiment North Carolina Troops.* This exhaustive work was an indispensable reference in supplementing the sometimes confusing narration of John Wesley, as well as for many contextual details of his service. His personal service record — including enlistment, hospitalizations, wounds, furloughs, and parole at Appomattox — is preserved with the Confederate military records in the National Archives, Washington, D.C.

Record of a Soldier in the Late War

Preface

The following pages will be a brief record of my life and service as a soldier in the Civil War, and is written nearly forty years after the close of the same, and while I was confined to the bed with rheumatism in the year 1904.

Many things have passed my recollection, but I will try to leave a few on record to the best of my memory, at this time. The reader may wonder at this late day, with the rush and hurry of the world, and having but a very faint recollection of things that occurred back in the sixties, I should do so; but I will say that experience teaches and prints in the human mind many things that nothing else can, and it is not always the case that they are soon forgotten and especially so when life is at stake or some great trouble before us.

This sketch will be brief and not perfect in language, as I am not an educated man. I will pass over about four years of my life in a very brief way. I have said before, this was written the first part of the year 1904.

J. W. Bone

A member of Company I, 30th Regiment
North Carolina Volunteers

NORTH CAROLINA.

A CALL TO ARMS!!!

Ye sons of Carolina! awake from your dreaming!
The minions of Lincoln upon us are streaming!
Oh! wait not for argument, call, or persuasion,
To meet at the onset this treach'rous invasion!

Oh! think of the maidens, the wives, and the mothers,
Fly ye to the rescue, sons, husbands and brothers,
And sink in oblivion all party and section,
Your hearthstones are looking to you for protection!

"Her name stands the foremost in Liberty's story,"
Oh! tarnish not now her fame and her glory!
Your fathers to save her their swords bravely yielded,
And she never yet has to tyranny yielded.

The babe in its sweetness—the child in its beauty,
Unconsciously urge you to action and duty!
By all that is sacred, by all to you tender,
Your country adjures, arise and defend her!

"The Star Spangled Banner," dishonored is streaming
O'er bands of fanatics; their swords are now gleaming;
They thirst for the life-blood of those you most cherish;
With brave hearts and true, then, arouse! or they perish!

Round the flag of the South, oh! in thousands now rally,
For the hour's departed when freemen may dally;
Your all is at stake, then go forth, and God speed you!
And onward to glory and victory lead you!

Thompson & Co., Printers, Raleigh, 1861.

North Carolina—A Call to Arms!!! September 1861.
(Wilson Library, University of North Carolina / Chapel Hill)

1.

VOLUNTEERING

September 1861–April 1862

After a lapse of nearly forty years, feeling that my earthly existence is growing short, and believing that some day there will be an attempt made to get as near as can be a record of those that wore the Gray in the Late War, I will leave a broken record of about four years' service in that war and if the task is undertaken and my plain and brief outline is worthy of a place on the record, it may be had. It will be of no daring adventures, nor of prison troubles, but of going steadily forward, taking and bearing realities of a soldier in war, as I come to them. After so long a period, my body and mind both growing weak, there are many incidents that occurred and were once fresh in my memory that are now forgotten.

I was raised on a farm and was about eighteen years of age when the war broke out. My father lived in a community that had very few educational advantages, therefore my education was very limited. At that time I had traveled but very little, just out of Nash County a few times.

Realizing that the South was in dead earnest and hostilities becoming very warm in some places, and believing that sometime in the near future I would have to go as a soldier, about the first of September 1861 I volunteered at Nashville, North Carolina, for a period of twelve months under W. T. Arrington, as Captain.[1] It was here that I had the first oath administered unto me. How well I have remembered it unto this day. I was sworn in with three others, all strong able bodied men, except myself. I was healthy, but rather small and young. But long before the war had ended my three companions had passed away and left me.[2]

On the 10th of September we joined a regiment at Raleigh. Our Company was second of the 30th N.C.V. Our company numbered about one hundred men and the Regiment about one thousand.[3] Here we elected Frank M. Parker, of Halifax County, as Colonel and drew uniforms and canteens.[4] In a few days we got on the train into box cars and left Raleigh on Saturday evening. While we were waiting at the depot, many of the men had their canteens filled with whiskey to comfort them through the night, as we were carried slowly to Wilmington. Nothing very important occurred during the night, only the songs, oaths and cheers of the men.

On Sunday morning about nine o'clock, we were pulled into Wilmington, N.C., and got off under the big car shed at the bank of the Cape Fear river; this was our first time with all the Regiment. The reader may imagine, but cannot realize at this point our situation. As I have said, we numbered one thousand men; many at this time were greatly under the influence of whiskey and were where they could get plenty more. We were sleepy, tired and hungry, and were off to war. We wanted to fight and the enemy not being very near, some did fight one another. On this present occasion many were put under guard and were guarded by the sober ones. The patience of good and moral officers was tested at this point. I very well remember a very good and moral officer use oaths on this occasion.[5] The men got quiet after awhile and we remained there all day and were given quarters that night in a long building.

The next morning we marched out near Oakdale Cemetery, and cleaned up a camp ground and stretched out tents.[6] We now came down to squad and Company drill and guarding camps. It was here that we drew our arms and ammunition.[7] We could

Confederate troops depart by train for the first Battle of Manassas.
(British Library)

now begin to keep step with drum and began to feel like we were
soldiers. We were having a very good time here, but did not realize
it, though we did later on. We had but little sickness, as yet. After
a few weeks stay here we were ordered down the Cape Fear River
to Smithville, now known as Southport, near the old historic Fort
Caswell.[8] We were stationed here to guard the inlet from the main
ocean to the river. We cleaned up drill ground near the edge of the
little town and began to get down to business.

   It was here that our brave Col. Parker came to us, he being sick
when elected, and took command of the Regiment. Here also, Rev.
A. D. Betts was commissioned as Chaplain and remained with us
until the close of the war, and was a good and faithful Chaplain.[9]

   Disease, also, set in on us, such as measles, mumps, yellow
jaundice, and many other things due to camp life.[10] Many of
the men died. I was taken with measles and was carried to the

Col. Francis M. Parker, commander of the 30th Regiment.
*(From the Francis Marion Parker Papers, No. 04896, Southern Historical
Collection, Wilson Library, University of North Carolina at Chapel Hill)*

hospital. I believed at that time, that it was almost certain death
to be carried to a hospital and did not want to go, but my captain
prevailed with me to go, assuring me that I would have better
treatment there than I could possibly get in camp.[11] The hospital
had been some kind of hotel, being about two stories high and the
rooms about twelve feet square.[12] The floor, with a blanket or two
spread down, and our knapsacks for a heading, was our bed, with a
blanket or two laid over us. The room that I was put into was filled
all around the sides of the wall about as thick as we well could lie
and all with the measles.[13] We had but few nurses, one or two to
the room and they were sent there from camp and did not want
to stay.[14] Our doctor would come around once or twice during the
day and night. Our diet was very poor for the occasion, and yet I
expect everything was nearly as good as the head authorities could

do, considering such a calamity having come on us at once, and not being prepared for it. As soon as a patient thought he could stand camp life again, the doctor would let him go. Many left too soon for their own good and I for one took cold in my head after I left the hospital, and can feel the effects at times yet.

The November winds had a very good sweep at our camp and made it very disagreeable for those that were convalescent. It was here that we lost the first man from our Company, he being my nearest companion, my playmate, school-mate, tent-mate, and one of the three who took the oath when I did.[15] He being older than I, and a very good boy, I could afford to take his counsel. I felt a great bereavement in his death.

I had about fully recovered, and was placed on duty one night when about eleven o'clock the roll sounded and there was a general stir in camp, whereupon it was learned that Col. Parker was ordered to have his regiment strike tent, pack and be ready to leave at an early hour the next morning for Port Royal, South Carolina.[16] The men on learning the meaning of the order, sang, hallooed, rejoiced, and had a jubilee at the thoughts of leaving the damp, desolate camp where we had passed through such a crisis.

At an early hour the next morning the boats were waiting at the wharf and we were going on board, but we soon learned that the 28th N.C. Regiment was to go to South Carolina as they were better disciplined than we were, and we were to take their place; they being camped about ten miles above us near Fort Fisher, at Camp Wyatt.[17] We sailed up the river to the camp and landed, and as we landed the 28th was ready to take our place on board and we took their place at Camp Wyatt. The camp and drill ground was already cleaned here, we only had to stretch tents. The camp lying between the Atlantic Ocean and the Cape Fear river, on a strip of land about one mile wide, with Fort Fisher at the end near the inlet, the wind had a fair sweep here and was nearly all the time blowing. The soil was nearly a sandy desert, so our situation here was not a very pleasant one at times.

There were two or three sand forts a few miles from the main fort, with a few large guns mounted on them.[18] There was a tall pole planted near Camp Wyatt, the height being sixty or seventy feet high, with attachments, so that it could be climbed. Every morning a boy would ascend to the top, with a spyglass and view the ocean and if there was one blockade vessel in sight there would be a white flag hung out on the pole; if there were two vessels in sight there would be two flags put out; if there were three or more, there would be a red one put out, so we had some idea of the number of blockade vessels that were watching the inlet.[19] One morning as one of these vessels came in cannon range of one of the sand forts, where two cannons were mounted, the officer in charge ordered the battery to fire on it, which it did. The vessel returned the fire and sailed off, this being the first time that any of the Regiment had heard a shot from the enemy, since its organization. It caused considerable excitement in camp.

A few days later, I was detailed as a guard and sent down to this fort to help protect it. I had to walk the beach to and fro for a hundred yards or so. At night, when not on post, my place for sleep was in the magazine with the ammunition. One night while I was asleep, the sentinel on post claimed that he saw a man walking on the shore and commanded "halt." When he did so the man ran and he fired at him. I was immediately aroused and in company with others followed for some distance, but did not see or hear anyone.

I was taken sick with fever at this fort and was sent to camp. After staying there some time with but little attention and getting no better, I was put on a four mule wagon, one evening and started to Wilmington, a distance of twenty to twenty-five miles by public road, and reached there sometime that night.[20] The trip was tedious and worrisome along the sandy road. I was carried to the hospital and remained awhile until I got some better. I then came home feeling that I had been gone a long time and had seen much of this world. After remaining at home a short while, I returned to my command at Camp Wyatt.

*A Corps of the Confederate Army Marching by Night
through Burning Woods.*
(Illustrated London News, *August 6, 1864*)

We spent the winter here in drilling, built winter quarters of
sawed lumber large enough for a company of one hundred to a
house, and went into them by companies. We had plenty to eat
of almost anything here and grew fat, lazy and restless. About the
last of the winter, it was seen by the head authorities that we were
getting very deep into war. So they passed a law, asking all men to
re-enlist for three years in the war, with the promise of fifty dollars
bounty and thirty days furlough, realizing that now was the time to
get the men into it before they learned the realities of war.[21] Capt.
Arrington, our Captain, was a man that had great influence with
his men, and as probably his would be the Company most likely to
re-enlist first, Col. Parker told Capt. Arrington that if his Company
would all re-enlist that he would let the whole Company go home
at once on a fifteen day furlough, and later on then could have the

other fifteen. The Captain went to work and with this inducement soon had every man re-enlisted. We soon packed the most of our baggage, firearms and ammunition down in our quarters, and bade farewell to our comrades and Camp Wyatt for awhile; it being the last time that most of us have seen it. This inducement helped the most of the other companies to re-enlist, but no other company was allowed to all go home at a time; this being about the first of March 1862. We reached our homes joyfully, which place many had not seen since the first of September, feeling that we knew a great deal about war, but really had not realized but very little, for excepting the sickness, we had had a very good time, better with many than home was, but we had about finished our "shortening bread" and it began to become tough.[22] We remained at home about twelve days.

Capt. Arrington received orders from Col. Parker for his command to join the Regiment at once, an attack being made at this time on New Bern. We soon left Nash County, and joined our Regiment at Wilmington. New Bern had fallen and the Regiment was stopped here.[23] We went into camp in the borders of Wilmington, our former camp, the one we left when we went to Smithville.[24] We remained here a short time and then moved out a few miles from the town and struck camp here. Here we done some picket duty along the shore. Nothing of much importance occurred here only we reelected officers, which made considerable changes both in commission and non-commission officers.[25] The alarm roll was beat here one night after we had all retired. Many of the men arose from their sleep under excitement; some had to be almost pulled out from their tents before they could be awakened; some packed and took their baggage in good form; some went with theirs hanging about them in a loose way; and some did not go at all, but the most of us soon formed on the drill ground. This was our first exposure to the enemy.[26] The Colonel complimented us for our promptness, but said let us do better next time and discharged us and told us to go back in our quarters. I mention such things to let the reader understand how ignorant we were of what was just ahead of us.

About the last of April, the 30th Regiment with a piece or two of Moore's battery were ordered to Jacksonville, Onslow County, a distance of nearly one hundred miles.[27] This was the first march of any considerable distance that we had been called on to perform since we had been in service. We started off in fine spirits, each one loaded with baggage. The roads were very sandy but we soon got upon a plank road, which helped us along in marching, but made our feet very sore.[28] We got to the end of the plank road the first day. The next morning we were about sore all over and several began to hire their baggage carried where they could. We reached Onslow County in a few days, very sore, worried and jaded, but this was war times and we felt that we were doing very good service. There were two companies of cavalry sent to us for picket duty, there being no enemy very near us, only as they raided through the country. We remained here for a few weeks, changed camps a few times and did some picket duty, and then broke camp and took up our march back to Wilmington again and struck camp in a few miles of the city, feeling very glad to get back, considering that we had rendered some good service and learned something of the art of war.

We have never known if our service was really needed in Onslow or if we were sent there to let us learn something of marching and to make us dispose of a lot of our baggage, which we did at the first opportunity. We remained here around Wrightsville Sound, until sometime in May, when we received orders to go to South Carolina.[29] We packed up and came to Wilmington and were again sent to our old camp to await further orders, making the third time we had occupied it in the course of eight months. We remained here until about the first of June. We were then ordered to report to headquarters at Richmond at once, it being about the time the battle was fought at Seven Pines.[30] We soon packed up and bid farewell to Wilmington and North Carolina. Many left both forever.

Notes

1 very warm: South Carolina seceded from the Union on December 20, 1860, followed by ten other Southern states. On April 12, 1861, the Civil War began when Confederate forces fired on the federal garrison at Fort Sumter, in Charleston Harbor, South Carolina. The first major battle of the war was fought near Manassas, Virginia, on July 21, 1861.   **Arrington:** William T. Arrington (1821–1862).

2 three companions: The regimental record shows that six others from Nash County enlisted the same day, September 10, 1861: Neverson Batchelor died of smallpox at Point Lookout, Maryland, February 1864; Hardy Bone died of pneumonia at Richmond, 1862; Singleton Langley died of wounds suffered at Malvern Hill on July 1, 1863; Josiah Parker died of disease in Charlottesville, Virginia, 1864. Joseph Vick was captured and paroled in 1865, and William B. Joyner surrendered in 1865.

3 Our company: Evidently to inspire esprit de corps, the companies were given names, such as "Brunswick Double Quicks" and "Duplin Turpentine Boys." Although JWB never mentions it, Company I was designated the "Ladies' Guards" (Taylor, 94).

4 elected: Although election of officers was limited to the second lieutenant rank after 1862, the system remained in place at the company level. Senior officers "unanimously disapproved of the elective system." However, "until almost the end of the war Confederate companies were repeatedly disorganized by these political campaigns for military office. . . . Confederate soldiers, liberty-loving citizens from a democratic society, cherished the right to elect their officers, and the politicians defended them." David Donald, "The Confederate as a Fighting Man," *Journal of Southern History* 25 (May 1959): 178–93, cited in Michael Barton and Larry M. Logue, *The Civil War Soldier: A Historical Reader* (New York: New York University Press, 2002), 181.   **Parker:** Francis Marion Parker (1827–1905), scion of a prominent Edgecome County family, in 1850 owned twenty-eight slaves and farmed three hundred acres in corn, cotton, wheat, and other crops. Like JWB, he was intensely religious, but unlike him, he was a fiery Confederate nationalist with an intense hatred of the enemy. He wrote to his wife on June 1, 1862, "Let us pray...that we may annihilate the invading devils. . . . I have perfect confidence that this will be done" (Taylor, 181).

5 moral officers: To JWB, that a moral person would use an oath (presumably something like "damn you") is evidence of extreme provocation.

6 Oakdale: Created in 1855, the sixty-five-acre Oakdale Cemetery was the first rural cemetery in North Carolina, laid out in Victorian style with a maze of curvilinear avenues winding through the hilly terrain. The drives were depressed and the plots raised, often behind masonry walls. The cemetery is about one mile from the Cape Fear River.

7 arms and ammunition: He might eventually have been issued a .58 caliber British Pattern 1853 Enfield rifled musket, weighing 9.5 pounds, a weapon imported by both sides, but this early in the war, a hodgepodge of old muskets was commonly pressed into service by state regiments. During the war, an American version of the Enfield was built in North Carolina and Louisiana. The Massachusetts-made Springfield Models 1855 and 1861 musket, of similar design and weight, were issued to U.S. forces, but many were later picked up by Confederates on battlefields. He also would have received a leather cartridge box with a shoulder strap, which normally contained about ten lead minié balls, or bullets. A cap box, worn on a belt, held the percussion caps — that is, the powder charges. A bayonet, if he had one (none is mentioned in the memoir), would have been carried in a scabbard on the belt.

8 Smithville, Fort Caswell: Now called Southport, this town is twenty-two miles from Wilmington at the mouth of the Cape Fear River. Fort Caswell is across a marshy inlet about two miles from Southport. The fort was completed in 1836. It changed hands four times during the war.

9 Betts: Alexander Davis Betts (1832–1918), minister of the North Carolina Conference, Methodist Episcopal Church. He entered the service at Smithville, North Carolina. His wartime diary, *Experience of a Confederate Chaplain, 1861–1864,* W. A. Betts, ed. (Chapel Hill: Academic Affairs Library, University of North Carolina, 1996), was first published in 1906.

10 Disease, also, set in: Pneumonia, dysentery, measles, malaria, typhoid, and smallpox were rampant in army camps, especially in the early years of the war, and took a fearsome toll. Many epidemics were caused by fecal contamination of camp water supplies. Surgeons would use the same unsterile instruments on one wounded soldier after another, and many did not wash their hands, or lacked clean water with which to do so. While there was some understanding that cleanliness was associated with recovery from disease, it was difficult or impossible to enforce a sanitary regimen in the army. "Altogether, two-thirds of the approximately 660,000 deaths of soldiers were caused by uncontrolled infectious diseases," writes J. S. Sartin, "and epidemics played a major role in halting several major campaigns. These delays, coming at a crucial point early in the war, prolonged the fighting by as much as two years." "Infectious Diseases During the Civil War: The Triumph of the 'Third Army,'" *Clinical Infectious Diseases,* April 1993, 580–84. Confederate medical officer Joseph Jones estimated that of the approximately 600,000 Southerners in action, "on the average each one of these fell victim to disease and wounds approximately six times during the war." H. H. Cunningham, *Doctors in Gray: The Confederate Medical Service* (Baton Rouge: Louisiana State University Press, 1958), 3. The role of germs (even less that of mosquitoes) in infectious disease and sepsis in wounds was not understood until the experimental work of Louis Pasteur and Joseph Lister became known after the war. Ira Rutkow writes, "That the Civil War occurred in the waning years of medicine's prescientific era heightened its tragedy. Physicians were essentially helpless when confronted with communicable illnesses and devastating wound infections. Yet within one decade of the war's end, an understanding of the role of microorganisms in producing disease and the principles of antiseptic surgery would become accepted everyday knowledge." Ira M. Rutkow, *Bleeding Blue and Gray: Civil War Surgery and the Evolution of American Medicine* (New York: Random House, 2005), 317.

11 hospital: JWB's fear was not unusual or unjustified. "The mid-nineteenth-century hospital was viewed by society as a lower-class institution. Most were attached to the local alms house and were in deplorable condition. . . . No decent member of society would consider hospitalization." Rebecca Barbour Calcutt, *Richmond's Wartime Hospitals* (Gretna, La.: Pelican Publishing, 2005), 13.

12 some kind of hotel: General Hospital No. 4 in Wilmington, a brick building with two hundred beds on the corner of Dock and South streets, was formerly the Seamen's Home and had been used as a hotel. Many such buildings were hastily adapted to accommodate the masses of wounded. The scale of battle casualties had not been foreseen by either side, and there were few real hospitals as understood today.

13 thick as we could lie: The likelihood of further spread of the disease among those not immune, given the proximity of patients and the poor sanitation, would have been high.

14 but few nurses: Nursing care in the modern sense did not exist. There were no training programs in nursing in medical schools and no diploma-issuing nursing schools. The first nurse-training program, a six-month course, was set up by the Women's Hospital of Philadelphia in 1869, followed by more extensive "Florence Nightingale Schools" in the following decade. It is not clear who these people are who JWB says "did not want to stay," but they clearly are not what we would think of as nurses.

15 playmate: Even though JWB is deeply grieved at this loss, the boyhood play-mate's name is not revealed, nor are those of any (other than Singleton Langley) of his comrades.

16 Port Royal, South Carolina: About two hundred miles south of Wilmington, between Charleston, South Carolina, and Savannah, Georgia.

17 Fort Fisher: Fort Fisher was the largest earthen fort in the Confederacy. It protected the vital trading routes of the port at Wilmington, North Carolina, from 1861 until its capture by Union troops in 1865. Wilmington was one of the most important points of entry for supplies for the Confederacy. Colonel Seawell

L. Fremont of the 1st N.C. Volunteer Artillery and Engineers was commander in 1861. He added four batteries to the fort. By 1864, 2,400 Confederate troops were stationed at Fort Fisher, fortified with twenty-two guns and two large batteries at each extreme for sea defense, and twenty-five guns on mounds for land defense. On January 15, 1865, 8,000 Union troops attacked over land, taking Fort Fisher in a six-hour battle. Today Fort Fisher is a national historic landmark. **Camp Wyatt**: A Confederate training site north of the artillery battery at Fort Fisher, located on a narrow stretch of dunes across the Cape Fear River from Southport, seventeen miles from Wilmington. Named for Private Henry L. Wyatt of the 1st North Carolina (Bethel) Regiment, believed to have been the first Confederate soldier killed in action.

18 sand forts: makeshift fortifications, composed largely of sand, constructed in oceanfront areas, as distinct from permanent forts of earth, brick, or stone.

19 blockade vessel: The Union blockade at the mouth of the Cape Fear River was intended to prevent supply ships from reaching the Confederate position at Wilmington. It consisted of three main blockade lines. Out at sea, blockade vessels patrolled, looking for ships headed to Wilmington. A middle line of ships was closer to the inlet. Bar tenders were stationed off the shoal waters and ventured close to shore at night.

20 four mule wagon: For much of the war, this would have been the usual mode of Confederate evacuation. "The wounded usually underwent a most uncomfortable trip even when ambulance transportation was available. . . . Some spring vehicles were supplied early in the war, but when these broke down they were replaced by ordinary wagons, and as the latter moved over rough, wooded country or on roads rutted by artillery and army supply trains the occupants experienced a rude jolting. . . . Drivers were not always considerate of their charges, and one officer related that he was compelled to draw his pistol on one to stop him from traveling at breakneck speed over the roughest roads" (Cunningham, 120–21). Ambulance service improved, but eventually "collapsed for want of the necessary equipment and supplies." *Medicine of the Civil War* (Rockville, Md: National Library of Medicine, 1973), 3. Even in the far-better-equipped and -financed Union army, not until passage of the Ambulance Corps Act of March 1864 — a measure long opposed by Secretary of War Edwin Stanton — was a trained ambulance service established (Rutkow, 297).

21 passed a law: The Bounty and Furlough Act, passed December 11, 1861, provided that men could join the branch of service they preferred, and that if they did not like the company they were in, they could move to another. The law was a failure. On April 16, 1862, the Confederate Congress passed a conscription act — more than a year earlier than the United States — applying to men between ages eighteen and thirty-five. Fiercely resented and opposed by several states, it required a three-year term and automatically extended any current enlistment to three years. JWB reenlisted freely, apparently with no thought of doing otherwise, and was in for the duration.

22 shortening bread: A simple fried bread made with cornmeal, flour, eggs, and shortening. In this reference, JWB means the soldiers would have few pleasures after these days at home.

23 New Bern: Eighty-five miles northeast of Wilmington. Confederate troops at New Bern numbered 4,500 but were untrained and poorly equipped. On March 14, 1862, Union general Ambrose Burnside, commanding 12,000 men, stormed into New Bern. After a four-hour battle, the Confederates were overwhelmed and ordered to retreat by the inexperienced General Lawrence Branch. By December 1862, 20,000 Union troops occupied New Bern, a force larger than the combined Confederate units in the state of North Carolina.

24 our former camp: Oakdale Cemetery, Wilmington.

25 reelected officers: After the conscription act, men who reenlisted were allowed to vote again for their officers; however, three out of four were voted out. At senior ranks, writes Joseph T. Glatthaar, "after that round of new elections, the government required promotion strictly by seniority, with the enlisted men able to vote only to fill vacancies at the second lieutenant's rank." *Soldiering in the Army of Northern Virginia: A Statistical Portrait of the Troops Who Served under Robert E. Lee* (Chapel Hill: University of North Carolina Press, 2011), 85.

26 first exposure: Since no enemy was in evidence, this seems to have been a surprise drill. Seven months after enlistment, the regiment clearly is still woefully unready for combat. JWB does not refer to firing or arms training, only marching.

27 Moore's battery: On August 23, 1861, the Wilmington Light Artillery was mustered into state service at Camp Boylan, near Raleigh, and designated Company E, 10th Regiment N.C. State Troops (1st Regiment N.C. Artillery). The official designation was used infrequently, and the battery was more often referred to as "Moore's Battery," commanded by Captain Alexander D. Moore. In October 1861, Moore's Battery was supplied with six brass cannon and sent to Wilmington.   **Jacksonville:** Fifty miles northeast of Wilmington. With no strategic or tactical reason to transfer troops to Jacksonville at this time, JWB's suspicion that the march was merely a training exercise seems justified.

28 plank road: A dirt path or road covered with wooden planks, required by law to be eight feet wide. Plank roads were considered a major improvement to create connections between seaports, railroad hubs, and centers of commerce. In the 1850s, approximately five hundred miles of plank road were laid in North Carolina. While practical for wagons drawn by teams of horses with shod hooves, the wooden boards were hard on human feet, especially if marchers were barefoot or wore thin-soled shoes.

29 Wrightsville Sound: A body of water between the mainland and outer barrier beach, about ten miles east of Wilmington.

30 Seven Pines: The Battle of Seven Pines, May 31–June 1, 1862, was the culmination of a Union offensive that put the Army of the Potomac on the outskirts of Richmond.

2.

GAINES'S MILL, MALVERN HILL
June–August 1862

We had now spent about nine months as soldiers, but only knew a very little of the life of a soldier or the art of war, as the reader will learn, if they follow me through the rest of the war. We were very certain that we now had to come down to business and so we did. We reached Richmond on Sunday morning and were marched into Capitol Square.[1] There we began to see men walking around with their arms in slings, others with empty sleeves and pant legs; this looked very sad to us, believing that we would soon be exposed to the same fate.

We remained in the city the rest of the day and that night. That evening there were some Yankee prisoners brought in from the front. The Northern army then being fortified in about four miles of Richmond, the Confederate Capital. On Monday morning we were marched out and assigned to a place in Lee's army, he then being Commander in Chief.[2] As we began to get out of the city and approach the regular army, we began to see men everywhere, their arms stacked and the artillery horses with their harness on them, all ready to move at a moment's warning.

Our Regiment now numbered upward of one thousand men for duty. As we passed through the camps, we were occasionally hailed in this way, say "Mister, what Brigade is that" somebody would respond, "it's no Brigade, it's the 30th Regiment." The reply would come back "the 30th what?" Then we would say "the 30th North Carolina." You see, we had known no other troops but North Carolina ones, while they were with some from every State in the Confederacy.[3] It was now tents, men, guns, artillery, and horses everywhere, drums beating, bands playing, and cannon firing on one side or the other at all times, nearly both day and night. There was a considerable change with us in the last three days. We were now assigned to Anderson's Brigade, D. H. Hill's Division.[4]

As soon as we had gotten into camp, we received orders to cook three days rations and be ready to march at a moment's warning, an order that we had not been used to. The weather being warm, our rations would soon spoil and we would have to throw them away. Nearly every evening the batteries on both sides would get to firing at each other and we would have to fall in with arms, ammunition, rations, and knapsack, and march to the fortifications, and sometimes remain there a part of the night.

We now began to see what a good time that we had while in North Carolina, and would have been glad to have gone back there, almost anywhere. But, oh, our soldier's life was not spent in our Native State. After we had been here a few days our Regiment was carried out and placed on picket duty at Seven Pines, near the enemy, this being the first time we had been close to the enemy. Therefore, several of the Regiment were under some excitement and would not speak louder than a whisper.

Fortunately for our Company, there had been two men transferred to us since our arrival from the 15th North Carolina Regiment. They had been in the battles of Williamsburg and Seven Pines and were under no excitement, but would laugh at those that were.[5] They were very nice and would answer our questions in regard to our situation. They would tell us that it was nothing but a picket line in front of us, which it was, and this gave us some relief to learn something more about our situation and a soldier's life.[6]

We were ordered that evening to advance upon the line, which we did in very good order for the first time, although great excitement prevailed with many.[7] In this attack Dr. or Captain Grissom got shot through the shoulder and he was the first man to get wounded in the Regiment by the enemy.[8] Later in the evening we were ordered to advance again and this time there were sharp-shooters put out in front of the Regiment of which I was one.[9] We were put a little in advance and came upon the enemy's line and drove them back with no little excitement. It was told on one man in our Company that when we were advancing he saw one of the sharpshooters and remarked, "yonder is a Yankee," and took aim and fired at one of the same Company that he belonged to. (Fortunately with no result.)

Another man saw a blanket rolled up and both ends tied together and remarked look what a bombshell.[10] The Yankees threw their knapsacks and blankets down and left them. As we fell back, one of the men being of greedy nature, commenced picking up blankets until he got an armful.[11] Then seeing one that looked some better, he threw his armful down and picked it up, and went a little farther and remarked, "Here's another mighty good blanket," threw down the one that he had and picked up that one, and continued throwing down and picking up until there were no more. It was said that his last blanket was no good.

We were held on picket line that night, with orders that if we saw or heard the enemy to fire on them. As soon as it began to get dark the men began to fire and it was kept up through the night at times and yet the enemy did not approach nor return the fire. We were told next morning that we had to stay on that picket line until we learned to keep less fuss, unless the enemy did advance upon us. The next night there was scarcely a gun fired, and the next morning we were relieved and went back to camp being very glad to get off picket duty; but were continually being called out to the breastworks every day.[12]

About this time, things were in readiness for the seven days fight and we were aroused one morning just after midnight and started to some unknown place.[13] We reached Mechanicsville sometime in the morning.[14] The troops were marching from different directions and stacking arms, and they were commanded to remain in place and be ready at a short warning.

In the evening we heard the ball open, as we called it, away up on our left; it being Jackson coming down from the valley and attacking in rear.[15] We were called in and marched to the front, and were shelled very heavy. Here the battle of Gaines Mill was fought.[16] We were not really engaged that evening, but had many shells to fall and burst around us. I recollect very well about dark one shell struck the ground just in front of me, throwing dust all over me, passing betwixt me and the next man on my left, wounding him and just missing me. We bivouacked on the field that night; the fighting and shelling nearly ceased after awhile, but the sharpshooters kept up a fire at times all night.[17] We were expecting to be called up at any time, so we slept with our outfit on and upon our muskets.

Early the next morning the battle was renewed and we marched forward and supported a battery, while it shelled the enemies.[18] We were exposed very much here, but I don't recollect that any of the Regiment was killed. Right here, I will mention one of the saddest looking scenes, at that time, that I witnessed through the war. As we advanced next morning to where a battery had been placed and operated, there laid a cannon dismounted and two dead men and a fine horse, with one hind foot shot off. These were the first dead people that I had seen that were killed. This was a sad looking scene to me and I felt then that I would be the next one. I heard others express themselves in the same way, but, oh, we did not dream of what was just ahead of us; this was just the beginning of sorrow.

We now had the enemy well routed, and they were on the retreat when we were after them as fast as we could go. The enemy leaving many things behind them, we pursued them for a few miles. When they reached Cold Harbor, they made a bold stand.[19] That evening the first battle at this place was fought.[20] We came

Battle of Gaines's Mill at Boatswain's Swamp (or Marsh),
June 27, 1862.
(Map by Hal Jespersen, www.cwmaps.com)

up, placed our artillery in position and commenced shelling. Our
Regiment was placed behind a battery in an open field to support
it.[21] The mid-day sun in one of the hot days of June sent its rays
upon us, but that was nothing to the shell, grapeshot and canister
shot that were poured down upon us from the enemy's batteries.[22]
Some were killed while others were wounded here.

After a few hours in this position we were ordered to go forward.
As we started the enemy fired their batteries upon us; it seemed that
they would kill every one of us but fortunately we soon reached a
small woods and continued to go forward until we came to a large
marsh.[23] When we reached it, we were ordered to fire into it; here
was our first fire in regular line of battle and it was a heavy one too,

but there were no enemies in there. The batteries continued to shell us and this was the place that the first man in our Company was killed. He was shot through the body with a musket ball and I have always believed that some of our men did it.[24]

I continued to load and fire, until I had orders to cease firing. I stopped and looking back of myself I saw a man sitting on the ground and firing regardless of where his balls went. The men of my Regiment ceased firing, according to orders from our Colonel. There came another Captain from some other Regiment along our line, ordering us to fire on, for the enemy was in the marsh. He was taken by the arm by a level headed private of our Company and told that we had orders to stop firing and for him to go to his own Regiment and command. I speak of these things to show how excitable some men are that ought to be level headed.

We now had orders to go forward. We soon reached a large open field, both sides were fighting through this field and we were ordered to charge, and charge we did. I will say right here, at the edge of this field, we had a commission officer and some others to stop and not go any further until the battle was over and this was the nearest that the officer ever got to battle. If he had gotten his just rights, he would have been Court Marshaled and dismissed; but we charged the enemy and took the field. They were fighting in every direction, but the firing soon ceased, as the enemy fell back and the victory was gained by the Confederates.[25]

Night was now on us and it was an awful one too. Men were lying dead, dying, groaning and calling for help in all directions. Men calling for their commands and it was a fuss that none can realize but those that have experienced such. We were again bivouacked on the battle field that night. I will again say that on this battle field there was a house and a woman whom remained in it during the battle.[26] The enemy had thrown its army betwixt her home and Richmond so she could not have gotten out if she wanted to. That morning both armies were away up at Gaines Mill fighting, but after awhile the Yankees came down the road in quick time and stopped and formed a line of battle on the lower side of the house; but at this time the Confederates came and formed a line of battle on the other side.[27] She perhaps was not aware of her situation, until the battle began; fortunately there was a cellar to the house and she stayed in it the battle out, without being hurt. Great many balls and shells struck the house.

The next morning we advanced a short distance and formed line of battle, but did not fight any that day.[28] That evening there was a detail made from the different regiments to go back on the battlefield and bury the dead. I was one that was detailed from our Regiment. We were furnished shovels and we went back and followed along where our Regiment fought, and as we would come to the dead men, we would dig a hole by their side and lay them in. If we could get a blanket we would spread it over them and then cover them with dirt. This seemed very bad to us, at this time, but this was war times, and we were regular into it now.[29] This being Saturday morning we remained here in line until Monday morning; there was fighting along the line every day, but we were not engaged until Tuesday evening at Malvern Hill.

We reached Malvern Hill on Tuesday just before twelve o'clock; fortunately for some of our Company there was a demand for some men to guard some prisoners.[30] Capt. Arrington hearing the order offered himself and Company as guard, which was accepted by the Colonel. We reported to the place, but the officer in charge of the prisoners seeing there were more of us than were needed took only about half of the Company and sent the Captain with the other part back to the Regiment. We joined the command and moved on for the battle; they were then cannonading on both sides and were getting the lines ready for action.[31] Our Brigade was placed in the center of the hill. It was high with a long slope; and a broad field below; most of the slope had a thick small growth upon it making it difficult to get through in good order.

We were the first to charge; we went forward through the broad wheat field (then a foot high) under heavy cannonading

Burial Crews at Bloody Lane after the Battle of Antietam,
September 17, 1862, by Frank Schell.
(Frank Leslie's Illustrated Newspaper)

until we reached the slope. We were then ordered to charge up
the slope which we did the best we could; the 30th Regiment got
through in very good order.[32] We were now almost at the top of
the hill, in a broad open field, where the enemy was located and
using all their artillery on us to the best advantage. I well remember, just as I reached the edge of the field, I heard a ball hit my left
hand companion and he fell dead. I soon had a ball shot through
my front leg.[33] We charged on until we got to the top of the hill;
here we had a broad view of the enemy and they had one of us. We
stopped and opened fire; it was a hot place, with lead and iron. In
the charge two of the regiments got so badly confused in going up
the hill, that they were in no order for the battle and did not do
very good service; this being the case, the enemy made their aim at
those most exposed. As I loaded and fired I could see the men fall
and hear them halloo all around me, but we held our line and kept
firing.[34] Finally I was wounded in the hand.[35]

About this time Col. Parker saw his situation and that his regiment was exposed so bad that he ordered a retreat.[36] On hearing this I made my way down the hill the best I could, expecting to be hit by a ball or piece of shell, but fortunately I was not. About the time I got down the slope a shell bursted over my head and a piece struck a member of my Company by the name of Singleton Langley and shattered his thigh.[37] I went to him and straightened out his leg and put a blanket under his head and left him to make the best of it that he could. I then went on and got with my Colonel and after more of the Regiment.

It was now getting late in the evening and they continued to send troops in. The fighting continued until a late hour that night, with heavy cannonading from the light artillery and from the gun boats in the James River. People here in Nash County said that they heard the cannons that night a distance of one hundred and fifty miles. The shells that were thrown from the gunboats were thrown a distance of five miles and were near the size of a big nail keg.[38]

Col. Parker got as many of his Regiment together as he could; it was then getting dark and they were scattered from the retreat. We assembled back in a forest of trees, near the place where we formed our line of battle before we made the charge. We were not called into action any more that night. We remained in the forest all night and were exposed to heavy cannonading as long as the fight continued. Many shells exploded over us cutting off tree branches and their tops, killing and wounding the men; it was an awful situation, as long as the artillery continued to fire. Sometime after it ceased, it commenced raining, and rained the rest of the night and the greater part of the next day.

Next morning everything was wet and things were somewhat better; it was then that I learned that Capt. Arrington, with some others of the Company were killed and several of them were wounded. The rest of our Company came up that was detailed the day before. They missed being in the hard fight by being detailed. This was a sad morning to those that were living for we were in a

The Battle of Malvern Hill.
(*Harper's Weekly*)

sad condition. That morning I found that I was not able for service on account of the wound that I had received the day before, so the Colonel sent me back to the rear. It continued to rain, and there were wounded men everywhere along the road and many lying beside the road. The enemy was now falling back to the gunboats and we dared not to go any nearer. This was the end of the seven days' fight.[39]

Our army remained here a week or so before going back to our old camp near Richmond. It continued to rain until the evening. I was about as wet as I could be, as well as being wounded and hungry, for I don't know how long it had been since I had taken anything to eat. In the evening we got an ambulance and driver and put Langley in it. I got on and some others that were wounded, also the nurse and we started for Richmond in the first part of the night; those that were wounded were taken to the hospital, and I

was given a bunk, but nothing to eat, as it was past supper time.[40]
I got on my bunk and wrapped up, for I was as wet as if I had been
dipped in water. This was the first night's rest that I had had in a
long time.

The next morning I got up and left the hospital and went out
to the camp where a few of our Company was, who did not go
into battle for different causes. I now got myself something to eat,
and began to give my wound some attention.[41] I went back to the
hospital occasionally to see Mr. Langley, but he died in a few days,
and his last words were, "that he was willing to face death." (He
was a good man.) His remains were sent home, and also Capt.
Arrington's. The death of Capt. Arrington was a great loss to his
Company as well as to the Regiment, for he was liked by nearly
all and was a brave man. First Lieutenant J. I. Harris now became
Captain.[42]

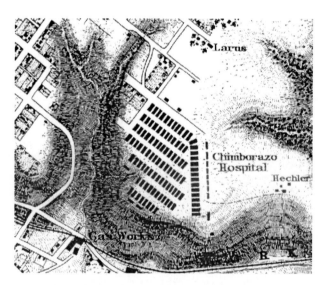

Map of Chimborazo Hospital, Richmond,
showing rows of low buildings, about 1865.
(National Park Service)

Notes

1 Sunday morning: June 8, 1862.

2 Commander in Chief: General Robert E. Lee (1807–1870) was not commander in chief at this stage. He was given command of the Army of Northern Virginia, one of several Confederate armies in the field, on June 1, 1862, replacing the wounded General Joseph E. Johnston. He was given command of all Confederate forces on January 31, 1865.

3 every state: The Confederate Army — like its Union counterpart — remained relatively localized, with soldiers from a state commanded by officers from that state, wearing their own uniforms. Many governors tried to maintain control of their states' forces, even resisting conscription. There was also a strong effort by governors to have soldiers treated in hospitals run by medical officers from their own states.

4 Anderson's Brigade: Commanded by General George T. Anderson (1824–1901) during the Seven Days' Battles of June 25–July 1, 1862.   **D. H. Hill's Division:** Commanded by Major General Daniel H. Hill (1821–1889), it saw action at Seven Pines and the Seven Days' Battles.

5 Williamsburg: Fifty miles southeast of Richmond, the Battle of Williamsburg was fought on May 5, 1862, and was the first battle of the Peninsula Campaign, in which 42,000 Union troops and 32,000 Confederate troops were engaged.

6 picket line: A line of soldiers posted outside an army's main line to provide early warning of enemy attacks.

7 advance upon the line: Attack the enemy's line.

8 Grissom: Dr. Eugene Grissom (1831–1902) of the 30th Regiment Infantry, Company D.

9 Sharpshooters: Unlike pickets, sharpshooters (what today would be called snipers) were usually specially trained and equipped marksmen assigned to kill enemy soldiers and officers at long range. The most famous were Berdan's Sharpshooters on the Union side, composed of men from several states, whom the 30th Regiment would face at Malvern Hill. They were hated and feared, and by many on both sides regarded as cold-blooded killers. Winslow Homer's 1862 magazine woodcut *A Sharp Shooter on Picket Duty* (later reworked as Homer's first oil painting) shows a sharpshooter in a tree, aiming a scope-equipped sharpshooter's rifle. Homer wrote years after the war that "it struck me as near murder as anything I could think of in connection with the army & I always had a horror of that branch of the service." Winslow Homer to George G. Briggs, February 18, 1896, Winslow Homer Collection, Archives of American Art, Smithsonian Institution. Since sharpshooters were specialists and did not come into organized Confederate use until 1863, and JWB seems to have had no special training in marksmanship, it may be that he is referring here (and later on) to skirmishers — a line of infantry placed in the vanguard of an advancing force to probe and harass the enemy, or to give early warning of his advance. Given that JWB never mentions skirmishers — a basic part of a battle formation — it seems likely that this is what he means.

10 bombshell: the green soldier apparently mistakes a suspiciously folded and tied blanket for some kind of explosive booby-trap; or perhaps it just looked like an artillery shell.

11 greedy nature: JWB will often note incompetent or unsoldierly — as well as admirable — behavior by other soldiers. While he admits to his naïveté in these early stages, he does not seem to have on his own conscience any behavior that would merit criticism, at least none that he cares to mention.

12 breastworks: Not a trench, but some kind of chest-high barricade for soldiers to fight behind and defend.

13 seven days fight: The Seven Days' Battles were fought near Richmond. They included the Battles of Oak Grove, Mechanicsville (Beaver Dam Creek), Gaines's Mill, Savage's Station, Glendale, and Malvern Hill. Historians identify them as distinct military operations, but for the average soldier the days and locations could all run together. JWB's recollection is not always consistent with the historians' view. However, his feelings and observations are true to the scene.

14 Mechanicsville: The brigade reached this community, seven miles northeast of Richmond, in the morning of June 26, 1862.

15 Jackson coming down: Whatever firing JWB is hearing was probably not Jackson, since he had not yet joined the fighting.

16 Gaines Mill: JWB is conflating separate engagements. Gaines's Mill was fought on June 27. The fight that began June 26 was Beaver Dam Creek (sometimes called the Battle of Mechanicsville). It began at three p.m. when General A. P. Hill attacked Union forces under General Fitz John Porter. Stonewall Jackson's forces arrived in late afternoon after a long, slow march from western Virginia but did not participate in the battle. Hill's attack against dug-in infantry supported by artillery was a failure.

17 bivouacked: Slept in the open.

18 early next morning: June 27.

19 Cold Harbor: A village about seven miles east of Mechanicsville.

20 first battle: In the Battle of Gaines's Mill on June 27 (sometimes called the first Battle of Cold Harbor), Jackson again was slow to participate, not getting his men into action until evening. The Confederate force of 57,000 finally broke the Union lines and forced a retreat. Nearly 1,500 Confederates were killed. In

May and June 1864, another battle was fought at Cold Harbor, with a disastrous frontal assault by Union forces under Ulysses S. Grant.

21 support it: A slow-moving artillery unit, with heavy cannon and caissons drawn by teams of horses, would be vulnerable to attack on the battlefield and would need to be supported by infantry.

22 shell, grapeshot and canister: Three types of artillery rounds. Shells were projectiles loaded with explosive designed to burst after firing. Grapeshot consisted of nine metal balls in a connected cluster. The much more effective and deadly canister round was a thin metal can, about one-and-a-half times as long as a modern coffee can, filled with twenty-seven smaller balls. A twelve-pound Napoleon cannon — the most common field artillery piece — firing grape or canister was like a giant shotgun, with devastating effect on unprotected infantry.

23 a large marsh: Boatswain's Marsh or Swamp, a stream tributary to the Chickahominy River. Since Gen. George B. Anderson's brigade was farther back from the enemy than other units (see map, p. 24), JWB might have seen no enemy (entrenched on high ground beyond). However, there was vicious fighting with heavy casualties in this area.

24 our men: The reason for this opinion is unclear. Possibly because he has not yet seen enemy infantry, he concludes that the bullet must have been from the Confederate side.

25 by the Confederates: It was a dearly won victory, with 8,300 dead and wounded Confederates and 6,800 on the Union side. JWB reports openly the confusion and ineptitude of the men. It is the only place where he condemns the behavior of an officer.

26 again say: He has not mentioned it previously. This is the first of two digressions about women caught in the fighting. They do not advance the narrative but reflect his disturbed reaction to the uncontrollable effect of mass warfare on innocent civilians.

27 quick time: A military rate of march, normally about 120 steps to the minute. Perhaps he only means that they were hurrying.

28 next morning: Saturday, June 28.

29 very bad: He hasn't the words to express his feelings at this grim duty, having first seen battle dead only two days before. The burial party apparently does not attempt to identify the dead; there was no official identification system — no "dog tags," which were introduced in the United States Army in 1906. Also, they had no way, and no time, to mark the grave sites.

30 Malvern Hill: Tuesday, July 1. About fifteen miles south of Cold Harbor and twelve miles southeast of Richmond, Malvern Hill rises slightly above the surrounding land. The hill slopes gradually down on the north side to an open field. Beyond, the terrain is swampy and thickly wooded. Today the topography is almost exactly as it was in July 1862, making Malvern Hill one of the least-changed battlefields of the war.

31 both sides: Artillery of both armies.

32 ordered to charge: The implication is that the force went from the woods through the wheat field at less than a charge, possibly double time, then charged where the ground inclined upward. A charge was a rush, but a slightly built man such as JWB, carrying a ten-pound musket and other gear, would not have moved uphill at great speed.   **in good order:** Union troops were positioned on the hill, facing north across the open field, aided by between thirty-one and thirty-eight cannon, many loaded with canister shells.

33 front leg: Apparently through the cloth of his pants leg only, since he reports no leg wound and continues charging.

34 see the men fall: The attack was confused and uncoordinated. Union sharp-shooters were picking off individual soldiers, while canister shells exploding in the ranks had the effect of making men seem to disappear. General Daniel H. Hill later said of the order to charge uphill over open ground against massed cannon, "It was not war. It was murder."   **held our line:** The regiment has stopped charging, formed a line, and begun firing uphill.

35 wounded in the hand: It is not clear which hand.

36 ordered a retreat: Parker wrote after the war that the enemy artillery line was only three hundred yards away. This exposed position could not be sustained. When he discovered that only the 30th and part of the 14th N.C. regiments had answered the call to charge, he ordered a retreat (Parker, 498).

37 Langley: Singleton Langley (1821–1862) enlisted the same day as JWB. Nelson Bone, JWB's grandfather, had purchased 113 acres of land from him in 1846, which suggests that he was well off. At age forty, he could have avoided service. Langley is the only soldier in the memoir, other than officers, whom JWB identifies by name, which may indicate the respect in which he held him, as someone of his father's generation.

38 gunboats: Three gunboats were anchored in the James River, about a mile behind the Union line, hurling fifty-pound shells. However, they were inaccurate and had little effect; indeed, they were feared as much by the Union side.

39 seven days' fight: Confederate dead and wounded at Malvern Hill were about five thousand. In contrast to his earlier swagger and eagerness to whip the Yankees, Parker was chastened. "What can make people go to war?" he wrote to his wife. "To witness the destruction of life on a battlefield is enough to put a stop to all such arguments for its future. I mean such arguments as war" (Taylor, 196). Total Confederate losses in the seven days were 20,141; Union losses were

15,849. With strong naval support, the Union position at Harrison's Landing was judged by Lee to be impregnable. Eventually, the Union army was evacuated by steamer.

40 taken to the hospital: He was admitted to Chimborazo Hospital No. 4, with "gunshot wound, hand," on July 2. Built on Chimborazo Hill, a bluff overlooking the James River on the east side of the city, it was the largest military hospital in the Confederacy, treating 76,000 wounded men in seventy-five to eighty wards in rows of low buildings, demolished soon after the war. Today it is the site of the Chimborazo Medical Museum, part of the Richmond National Battlefield Park.

41 wound some attention: Since it is mentioned in his service record, the wound was at least examined, but JWB does not report any treatment. It was evidently not serious, given that he attended to Singleton Langley, left the hospital the day after admission, and never mentions the wound again.

42 Harris: James I. Harris (1834–1864) enlisted September 10, 1861, at age twenty-seven. Elected first lieutenant April 1862. Promoted to captain July 1, 1862. Killed at Spotsylvania Court House May 12, 1864.

3.

FREDERICKSBURG

August 1862–April 1863

In a short time Lee's army returned to Richmond and went into camp. General Anderson was our Brigade General. He was wounded and died, and then D. H. Hill was our Major General.[1] We were now assigned to Stonewall Jackson's corps, but Jackson soon left us, taking most of his corps with him, and went to Orange C. H., Virginia, where he commenced fighting Pope's army.[2] General McClellan's army went forward to meet them, but they fell back to their boats.

We again went back to our camps, near Richmond, and remained until sometime in August, when Lee broke camp and took up the march for Jackson, then near Culpepper C. H., Virginia, a distance of one hundred miles or more.[3] On this march D. H. Hill's division was stopped between Richmond and Orange C. H. to watch the movements of McClellan, as his army was leaving the James river and making for Pope, then near Manassas, and to keep his troops from coming in between Lee's main army and Richmond; it was believed that all danger was passed, and the enemy was uniting with Pope and Banks near Manassas.

We were ordered to join Lee's army as soon as we could; it then being near Culpeper C. H., with Jackson. General D. H. Hill's division broke camp and started at once. We marched on for a few days, the weather being very warm, and I among many others

Confederate General Daniel H. Hill.
(National Park Service)

began to get sick.[4] I got so sick that I could not keep time in ranks. (We were required to make good time.) They gave me permission to march in the rear, but I continued to get worse. In a day or two I had gotten behind my Regiment. I reached Orange C. H., Virginia, one morning, the Regiment camped there the night before and left early the next morning for Manassas; that being the day the great battle was fought, known as the second battle of Manassas.[5]

When I reached the station, I was so sick that it did not seem that I could go any further, so I laid down at the station, some of my comrades with me; they brought me a loaf of bread, and advised me to get on the first train that left, and go to some hospital for treatment. I laid there for some time, and considered the matter over. (I still dreaded the idea of going to the hospital.) After cooling and resting awhile, I decided that I would go on and try to overtake my command, hoping that I might get some better.

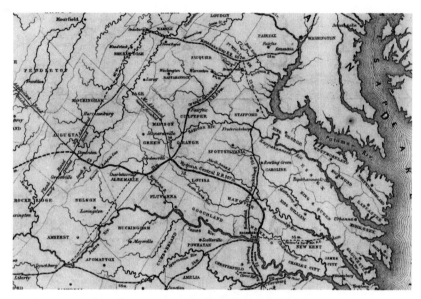

Virginia railroads in 1852, including the east-west Virginia Central
and north-south Orange and Alexandria.
(Library of Congress)

I started again along the Orange and Alexandria railroad, and
as I traveled that evening I saw a house some distance away (people
did not live very thick along here) and I decided I would stop
there, with the hope of getting some refreshments, but could not
get any.[6] Here I learned that the battle of second Manassas had
been fought that day. (My command did not reach there in time to
take a part in it.)[7] I now started back for the road, dark was coming
on, and I was by myself and felt that I was in the low grounds of
sorrow. I was in a low flat field, it being grown up in large weeds,
and I decided to stop and spend the night here, so I spread my
blanket down in this desolate place to spend the night.[8]

I now thought my situation over; here I was sick, worried,
further from home than I had ever been before and on my way
perhaps to battle, and might never return any more, no friend or
relative near me, and in a desolate place, and knew not where I

was going. My situation perhaps was as hard to me as Jacob's was the night that he wrestled with the angel, although if the angel was present she was not visible to me, and I took a very good night's rest, considering my condition and situation.[9] I was now beginning to learn to sleep and rest almost anywhere and in any situation, when I got an opportunity.

The next morning when I awoke it was raining, and I arose, went to the road, and soon found a wood pile that I sheltered under. I had gotten myself an ear or two of green corn, which I roasted and took my breakfast from.[10] After awhile, the rain stopped and I continued my march, feeling some better than I did the day before, so I kept traveling. Sometime during that day I overtook my comrades that left me the day before at that station. (They delayed more time than I did from the rain.)

We now journeyed on together and this made me feel a little more encouraged by finding them. On our journey we passed through the bloody battlefield of Manassas. Our men were buried, but the Yankees were not; this was an awful scene.[11] There were so many dead men lying stretched on the field that we could tell where their line of battle was formed; this was very sad for a boy in his teens. With my former experiences to look upon, and not knowing that I might not meet with the same fate, I felt very despondent and blue, but this was war times and we must get used to almost everything.

The army was still in pursuit of the enemy and were on their way to the battle of Sharpsburg.[12] We followed on, hoping to overtake them. I was not well yet and was nearly barefooted. (My shoes not being good ones, when I left Richmond, but thought they would do.) I had been traveling a great deal on turnpike roads, which had about worn them out.[13] When we reached the Potomac river at Leesburg, where the army had crossed into Maryland, we were stopped by an officer placed there, with orders to let none cross that were sick or barefooted.[14] Therefore I was stopped and sent across the Blue Ridge Mountains to Winchester, Virginia.[15]

A Christmas Dinner. A scene on the outer picket line.
(Edwin Forbes [1839-1895], Library of Congress)

In the valley we were furnished tents and rations, and remained here until the fight was over and the army recrossed the river and camped on this side. We were now sent to our respective commands. By this time I had rested up and had gotten about well.

The army was now greatly reduced and was very hard up for clothes and shoes. It was now sometime in September 1862. We remained between Winchester and Harper's Ferry, doing picket duty and tearing up railroads, until about the first of December; about this time we received orders to leave, so we crossed the Blue Ridge at New Market Gap and made our way to Fredericksburg, Virginia, where the rest of the army had located, and the enemy on the opposite side of the Rappahannock River.[16]

We were a very hard looking set of soldiers, the men had lost, thrown away and worn out about all that they started from Richmond with in August, and as I have said before we did not get much besides our rations while in the valley. As we came out the weather was very cold, the ground frozen and many of the men were barefooted, with large cracks in their feet, and when we would get up in the mornings and start on those turnpike roads, the blood would run out of our feet. We could be tracked nearly all day by the blood from our feet. There were orders sent to each regiment one night, while we were in this march for every soldier that was barefooted to go to the butcher's pen, the place where the beef was killed, and cut off some pieces of the raw hides, make holes, and then take some strings and tie them to our feet. We did this, and it did very well for about a day, then it would get dry and hard and would rub the skin off wherever it touched, so we could not stand them, unless we got new ones about every night.[17]

We reached Fredericksburg, just before General Burnside's command crossed the river. Lee formed line of battle about four miles from the town, and when the line was completed it was several miles long.[18] We occupied what is known as Marye's Heights and mounted many pieces of artillery on it which made great slaughter of the enemy.[19] I remember seeing one of the cannons that was shot into after the battle. The greatest day of the battle was the thirteenth day of December. Our Brigade formed on the West side of the railroad near Hamilton's Crossing. It was an open field to Fredericksburg, a distance of about four miles. We could see the enemy before us, but not in range of our small army.[20] The cannonading was very heavy. I remember after we had formed line of battle and were advancing when a shell struck the ground just in front of us, just missing Captain Harris and me, and exploding, it wounded a man in our rear so bad that he died from the effects. We advanced some distance, halted and awaited for an attack, being all the time exposed to the cannonading and sharpshooters.

We remained in this position all day and night, and the next two following days and nights; it being very cold we suffered a great deal on account of being very thinly clothed and shoed. On the last day there came cold rain and hail. There was a council of war held

by the generals to consider whether there should be an attack made
by night. General Jackson was in favor of it, and secured white
bands for his men to wear on their left arm, so that they could tell
each other, but the other generals over ruled him. He said, "let us
drive them into the river," but the attack was not made.

The next morning the enemy had retreated across the river.[21] It
was then seen that we had missed an opportunity of giving them
another thrashing, and that Jackson was right, but there were
many who remained on this side to return no more. We were not
engaged into this battle with our small army, only our sharpshooters, and they were exposed very much to the shelling. We now
located not very far from this place and commenced preparing for
the winter, as it was getting to be very cold. We had some tents
given us, a small quantity of shoes and clothing, and we made the
very best use of them that we could for the present time.

We remained here through the winter doing picket duty on
the river. It was very cold most of the time, and some large snows
fell, most of the timber was cut off the land, and this gave the wind
a very fair sweep at us. Many were taken sick during the winter,
and the smallpox raged to some extent. During a large snow one
evening we got to snowballing the brigade as though we were in
battle, and had a very lively time of it; the snow being about one
foot deep.

About night the roll was beat and we were ordered to fall in
with everything we had. We marched out and went some distance
up the river, and occupied an old camp where some troops had
been taken and sent to North Carolina; it was in the night, cold
and snowy, and nothing scarcely to make a fire with; so we fared
very common, but we were getting use to such.[22] We remained
here a few days, and then returned back near our camps, and began
picketing again on the river.

I went with some others on picket duty on the river in the
town of Fredericksburg, and there was a big snow on the ground.
We remained here a few days, and were put under a large old

A Snowy Morning on Picket.
(Harper's Weekly)

shelter with one side walled up, with but very little to make a fire with. The river was about one-half mile wide, with land all cleared on the other side for a long distance; we being on the South side and had but little protection. Our duty was to walk on the bank of the river for two hours at a time, and this had to be repeated about three times during a night. It snowed again while we were here, and drifted very deep along the side of the river where we had to walk. I walked the beach at a lonely hour of the night, with the snow on each side to my waist, with cold northern winds, blowing for miles across the river with great power, but this did not matter for I had to stand it if I could for two hours and then be off under our shelter four and then go back again for two hours.

I remember being relieved one night by a man that was very thinly clothed, and when he relieved me he asked me for my overcoat. I hated very much to come out of it, but I did for I knew what a pill he had to stand for the next two hours. The officer in charge remarked, "you gave up your coat at a very hard time," but

I have never regretted it for the man got killed in the very next battle that we fought.[23] Such as this was very bad, but as I have said before we had to stand it if we could, and if we could not we must die trying. After our time was out, we were relieved and to our delight went back to camp. A few and but very few were allowed to go home on furlough. Col. S. D. Ramseur was now made our Brigade General.[24]

Notes

1 wounded and died: JWB makes it appear that Hill's promotion followed Anderson's death. In fact, Hill was appointed major general in March 1862. Anderson died of wounds suffered September 16–17, 1862, at the Battle of Antietam.

2 Pope's army: John Pope (1822–1892), Union general commanding the U.S. Army of Virginia. In the summer of 1862, Lee and Jackson outmaneuvered Pope's troops at Manassas Station and the Second Battle of Bull Run, August 28–30, 1862. Pope was relieved of his command in September 1862.

3 one hundred miles: The distance from Richmond to Culpepper, Virginia, on today's roads is about ninety miles.

4 to get sick: The sickness, his fourth in the first year of the war, is not specified, but it appears to include high fever.

5 second battle of Manassas: The Confederate name for the battles of Bull Run.

6 Orange and Alexandria railroad: JWB is walking in a northeasterly direction along the track. The main Virginia railroads were the Orange and Alexandria between Alexandria and Gordonsville, the Virginia Central from near Covington to Richmond, the Richmond and Danville between those cities, and the Petersburg and Roanoke between Petersburg and Gaston, North Carolina. There were also shorter linking lines. The South Side Railroad between Petersburg and Lynchburg played a key role in the retreat to Appomattox. The standard railroad reference, with text and maps, is Robert C. Black III, *The Railroads of the Confederacy* (Chapel Hill: University of North Carolina Press, 1952, 1998).

7 did not reach: Hill's division reached the scene on August 31, the day after the battle.

8 spread my blanket down: If he was lucky, he might have been issued a blanket rubberized on one side, to keep him dry as he lay on the ground. Later (see pp. 78, Spotsylvania, and 93, Staunton, just before the Battle of Cedar Creek), it seems that his blanket does offer protection from wetness and frost.

9 the angel: Jacob and the angel, Genesis 32: 24–30. JWB supposes an angel to be feminine. Despite his despondency, he never (at least in retrospect) reports any thought of deserting, which 103,408 Confederates did throughout the war, including more than 23,694 North Carolina men, by far the largest number of any Southern state (Lonn, 231). In January 1862, at least twenty-six men deserted from Company I, most of whom would have been known to JWB (Taylor, 233).

10 I roasted: The soldier's kit would commonly include a small frying pan, and JWB apparently has matches. It is unclear how he could have made a fire in the rain, unless he fashioned a lean-to or found shelter, or what he would have used for fuel.

11 Yankees were not: With the massive scale of violence and rapid movement of armies in the Civil War, in many cases the dead were left unburied — especially those of the enemy, but sometimes in defeat or withdrawal those of one's own side. When they were buried, enemy dead were typically dumped en masse in hastily dug pits. "Burying the dead after a Civil War battle," writes Drew Gilpin Faust, "seemed always to be an act of improvisation, one that called upon the particular resources of the moment and circumstance: available troops to be detailed, prisoners of war to be deployed, civilians to be enlisted" (Faust 2008, 65).

12 Sharpsburg: The Confederate name for the Battle of Antietam.

13 turnpike roads: He apparently means plank roads. His experience was common, writes Bell Irvin Wiley: "There can be no doubt that thousands of Rebs failed to participate in the fighting of September 16–17 because the condition of their feet made it impossible for them to march with their comrades. It may easily have been true that the difference between a victory and a draw for Lee at Antietam was his want of a few thousand pairs of shoes." Bell Irvin Wiley, *The Life of Johnny Reb: The Common Soldier of the Confederacy* (Baton Rouge: Louisiana State University Press, 1978), 108–22, cited in Barton and Logue, 117–18. The problem was not, however, simple lack of shoes, but also their condition, and the lack of socks. Barefootedness was sometimes preferable. According to a contemporary account, "Very few men had comfortable or fitting shoes, and fewer had socks, and, as a consequence, the suffering from bruised and inflamed feet was terrible. It was a common practice, on long marches, for the men to take off their shoes and carry them in their hands or swung over the shoulder." Carlton McCarthy, *Detailed Minutiae of Soldier Life in the Army of Northern Virginia, 1861–1865* (Richmond: C. McCarthy, 1882), 41–55, cited in Barton and Logue, 90.

14 Leesburg: Leesburg, Virginia, is eighty miles north of Orange Court House. **let none cross:** Besides their poor condition, another reason to block stragglers from crossing was that the Potomac was a de facto international boundary. Uncommanded men who crossed into enemy territory might not return and hence be lost to the war effort.

15 Winchester: Winchester is at the northern end of the Shenandoah Valley, about forty miles west. It is not clear whether he walked or was sent by train, nor whether he was alone or with others. Since he must have been weak from sickness and was "nearly barefooted," and a walk is not described, rail transportation seems likely.

16 tearing up railroads: Trackage between Virginia and Maryland, to impede possible invasion. The rail line from Winchester to Harpers Ferry continued north to Frederick, Maryland, and on to Baltimore. East-west lines in Virginia, as well as lines leading south, were critical to the war effort.   **New Market Gap:** Eighty-five miles west of Fredericksburg, New Market is situated at a geographic divide in Massanutten Mountain, connecting the Shenandoah Valley to the Page Valley.

17 every night: This improvisation became increasingly common. Cunningham cites "a circular issued to the Army of Tennessee late in 1864 which ordered field commanders to see that sandals were made from 'green beef-hides' for all barefooted soldiers" (175). According to Wiley, "The results were not satisfactory." One soldier "complained that his rawhide sandals, 'stretch out at the heel . . . whip me nearly to death they flop up and down they stink very bad and I have to keep a bush in my hand to keep the flies off of them'" (Barton and Logue, 117–18).

18 Burnside: Ambrose Everett Burnside (1824–1881) took command of the Army of the Potomac in November 1862. In his attempt to advance on and capture the Confederate capital at Richmond, he was badly defeated at the Battle of Fredericksburg, December 13, 1862. He was replaced in January 1863 by Major General Joseph Hooker.

19 Marye's Heights: The scene of a disastrous series of Union charges across open ground, where about eight thousand were killed or wounded.

20 small army: The brigade, including the 30th Regiment.

21 next morning: December 15.

22 fared very common: To be in poor circumstances.

23 very hard time: The officer's comment indicates what an unusual act this was. JWB's point seems not to be that he is a hero (he mentions no other selfless act of his own), but that while the duty was almost unbearable, to do anything but bear and share it was unthinkable.

24 Ramseur: Stephen Dodson Ramseur (1837–1864) took command of the brigade that included the 30th Regiment when George Anderson died from wounds suffered at Antietam. He graduated in 1860 from the U.S. Military Academy, commissioned a second lieutenant. He was promoted to brigadier general in November 1862 at age twenty-five, the youngest general in the Confederate army at that time.

4.

CHANCELLORSVILLE

May–June 1863

About the first of May 1863, General Hooker commenced moving his army across the river at Fredericksburg and near Chancellorsville.[1] The most of our army being camped around Fredericksburg. I was on picket duty at this time, just below the town, and was put forward as a sharpshooter to help check their line, as they advanced. After they had crossed the river we came in contact with the enemy and held them back, but were shelled, wounding some of our sharpshooters.[2]

We remained in line all day and night, and most of the army moved up the river and especially Jackson's corps. I was left down on the sharpshooters line, but early the next morning, May 2nd, we were relieved and sent on after our command in great haste; it then being some distance ahead, starting the day before.[3] We overtook our command that evening, and at this time they were getting near the enemy, and forming line of battle. We joined them, and advanced on the enemy driving them back and fighting until dark. The fighting nearly ceased, only the sharpshooters keeping up a fire at times through the night. We laid down in line of battle, where dark came on us, expecting to have to go forward at any time. With this expectation, the sharp reports from our sharpshooters, the line just in front of us, the report of cannon, and occasionally a shell bursting near us, our slumbers were not very long at a time through the night.

The next morning, as the artillery bugle sounded, and the mule brayed, we began to arise and say our prayers, expecting to have to go forward soon, and not knowing but this was the last morning that we might see in this world, but to our surprise the morning broke, the sun arose, and ascended up in the heavens, and no move was yet made. While in this condition, we were at a loss to understand our situation, but old Stonewall was not, he knew what he was about, and was planning to make one of his forward moves (a flank move).[4] In a few hours we were called to attention and marched back to the rear, then taken around through a thick wilderness of undergrowth, over brushes, logs, branches, and everything else that we came to and that in quick and double quick time, traveling a blind path. It being a warm day, the men began to get rid of some of their winter clothing and blankets, the way that we traveled being scattered with them. It seemed that we made fifteen or twenty miles in about two or three hours, finally we came to a halt in a thick woods, and formed line of battle, and went forward.[5] We soon rousted a gang of wild turkeys, then captured a cavalryman in the enemy's outpost, as a picket. He was greatly surprised and made no effort to get away. He said, "that he had no idea that there was a 'Johnnie Rebel' near him."[6] We continued to go forward, and continued to find Yankees. We would fire into them, and they would fall back, and form line of battle. We would advance on them, and they would fire and fall back. We continued doing this through the woods until dark came on. The enemy not making a very firm stand at any time; this part of the country did not seem to have ever been inhabited to much extent; the settlements being very scarce; this is the time we gained confidence in our Brigade General, as he managed us so well through the woods.

Dark came on and we stopped in line of battle, the enemy in our front. It was General Jackson's intention to continue the fight that night, as we all expected, but a little after dark there was a brisk skirmish fire in front, then all ceased. This is where Jackson got his death wound. He had ridden by our picket line, making

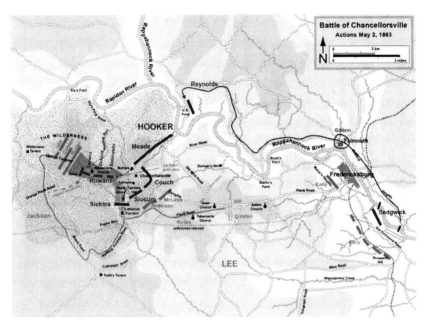

Jackson's flank march at the Battle of Chancellorsville.
(Map by Hal Jespersen, www.cwmaps.com)

arrangements for the attack, and as he rode back he was mistaken
for the enemy's cavalry, and fired on by some of his men, and mortally wounded, and died from it in a few days.[7]

This was sad news for his men, who had such great confidence
in him as a leader, but we learned nothing about it until the battle
was all over. It was a sad thing for the Confederacy. Some have
predicted that the South would have whipped had he lived, on the
grounds that he was such a Godly man.[8] The wounding of Jackson put a stop to the night attack, so we remained in line of battle
all night, and slumbered on our muskets, if slumber we did, and
I mean that we did, for we were exhausted and could rest almost
anywhere. Morning came, and we were aroused, more confident
of a hard battle than we were the morning before. About this time
the sun arose, and we were moved forward, it shined on many a

wounded soldier that morning for the last time. We continued to
go forward through a thick underbrush, with a very faint idea of the
deadly blow that would soon be showered upon us from our enemy.

About this time General Ramseur ordered Colonel Parker
to move his regiment to the right, and support Pegram's battery,
which was in danger at that time, and then to use his own judgment.[9] We supported the battery as long as the Colonel thought
best; we then moved forward to the support of a line of battle that
was in our front, then made an attack upon the enemy. During
the night, the enemy had piled up logs, thrown dirt upon them,
making very strong breastworks, cutting down the trees and undergrowth in front of the works, making it a bad place to get through.
The line of battle in our front reached the works, about this time
the enemy reinforced the works with fresh troops; at this point we
were about in sixty yards of the works making all the haste that
we could, and when getting into the tangled brush, the line in our
front was compelled to leave the works by being overpowered and
commenced retreating as they were coming out.

At this point Colonel Parker ordered his regiment to lie down,
which we did, until they passed us, then he ordered us to arise and
go forward. On getting near the works, the enemy left in great
confusion, and then using our opportunity to the best of advantage until they were out of range which was not very long.[10] At this
point we saw that we were fired upon from the right, there being a
space that was not covered by our troops, and they had not left the
works. We then turned our fire upon them and they fled in great
haste, leaving many of their companions behind them.

There was a battery in our front shelling us with all the force
that it had. We then went over to the breastworks and made a
charge through an open field, and the batteries were firing very
heavy upon us. The enemy had formed in rear of the batteries, but
not withstanding we went right on for the batteries. We began to
get in shooting distance, and the artillery men left their guns, and
the line of battle fled, leaving the field to us. We went so far in such

a short time that one of our batteries took us for the enemy and fired on us for a short time, until they found out better. It is said that we got near General Hooker's quarters before he left them.

We now made a stand near the Chancellorsville house (it being a large two story building on the Orange and Fredericksburg plank road and used as an inn for foreigners).[11] We were now on the East side of the plank road, the West side was a forest of timber, and it was then on fire. We were ordered to go at once and put the fire out, there being many of our dead and wounded subject to being burned. We moved our wounded and stopped the fire, but many of the dead bodies on both sides got burned before we could get control over the fire.[12] The battle had now about ceased.

We again formed line of battle on the east side of the plank road, and we now looked after our men to learn how many we had for duty. Our Company carried into the fight that morning seventy-five men, of that number forty were killed and wounded, eight being killed on the field.[13] Among the number killed was a very moral young man and a good soldier, who had a brother in the Company. In the morning before he started from our bivouac he wanted to give his brother his pocketbook and rations, for he said that he thought he would be killed that day. I did not know what had passed between him and his brother that morning, but noticed him as we advanced, he went straight forward, and did not seem to hear or regard orders until his attention was called the second time. We believed that through some vision of the night that he was satisfied that he would be killed that day. It was often times the case that we would have some soldiers say if they went in battle again that they would be killed, and when the next battle would be over they would be dead.[14] This was one of the hardest battles that we ever fought, and General J. E. B. Stuart was now in charge of Jackson's corps.[15] This was Sunday, May 3, 1863.

We remained in line of battle on the plank road, and watched the enemy to see what move they would make, and whether to attack them or not. On Monday it rained, that evening I was sent

out to the sharpshooters line for the night. We were expecting
an attack that night, so there was a strong line put in front and
another one just in our rear. I was in the front line. Sometime
that night the front line commenced firing on the right, as if the
enemy was advancing, and firing on down to the line where I was,
and they kept on by me. I could not hear or see any sign of the
enemy, but once in awhile I could hear some cannons fire. The
line in our rear commenced firing, and we in their front. While
this was our condition, our commanding officer ordered the front
line to fall back to the rear line which we did in quick order and
without much damage. Our officer being a profane man, the rear
line understood his meaning. The line that was in front was now
ordered forward to its former position.

At times in the remainder of the night there would fall heavy
showers of rain. We were now in the forest and the whippoorwills
would come near us and sound their clear notes, which would
attract our attention by reminding us of former days. We passed
through the remainder of the night without being disturbed very
much. When morning dawned, we were a very wet, sleepy, cold
and hungry line of sharpshooters, and as there were no great signs
of being attacked, we were hoping to be relieved and go back to
our commands in line of battle, where our chances would be some
better for a little refreshment, which we were in very much need.[16]
Our commanding officer received orders that we must advance on
the enemy's line and locate their situation in regard to an attack
upon them. Both lines were now thrown together making a very
strong line and we advanced forward.

As we started off, the enemy opened their artillery on us, being
loaded with grapeshot and canister shells which was not very pleasant to face, but we went forward until we drove the enemy's line
and they fired from their breastworks, and also from their batteries.
We were just in the edge of a woods, taking in the situation of their
lines, from the view it seemed as though a great many of our men
would be killed and a great number were killed. I remember a man

A canister shell with contents.
(Minnesota Historical Society)

who was lying very near to me, and all at once a cannon ball or shell struck his head and knocked it from his body.[17] After locating their condition we fell back to our former line and had grape-shot and canister shells thrown among them, but they made it so very hot for us that we retreated. It was then necessary that we should form our picket line. We found the enemy so well fortified that they were not attacked by the line of battle. We remained on our picket line until evening and then we were relieved, being greatly exhausted and for want of sleep and refreshment.

The next night the enemy recrossed the river and occupied the other side.[18] This night was the end of one of the hardest fought battles of the Confederacy. General Hooker having one hundred and fifty thousand men while General Lee had only fifty thousand.[19] Lee gained the victory but there was a great loss of men on both sides.[20] At this time I felt about as despondent as I had in any part of my life, after realizing things as they were; my relatives, tent mates, school mates and nearest comrades were gone.[21] I felt very lonely but thankful that I was spared after passing through the dangers that I had for the past few days, and feeling that I had discharged my duty faithfully as a soldier. During the fight I had been standing in the front, and did not decline to try to discharge my duty, and I realized too that the Supreme power had let me safely through this struggle and kept me safe from the dangers that I had been exposed to. Having these encouragements, I cheered up and tried to continue as a good soldier trusting to a higher power than man to lead me.

Right here I will mention an accident that occurred during the time of the fighting to show to the readers that women as well as men had to pass through great tribulation during these times of war. As I have said before, this country was partly a wilderness and not inhabited much. In this forest stood a small log house surrounded by a thick growth. This house was inhabited by a woman and three small children, the largest a girl and the youngest only a few years old. (Her husband was in the army.) On Saturday morning she found the meal low in the gum, and not enough to last her the following week.[22] Perhaps the woman had heard cannonading the evening before down the river, as she had heard many times during the past few months, but not aware there was a battle approaching, for she had not seen a soldier in some time in or around there.

Early Saturday morning she instructed the oldest to remain there and keep the children, while she went to a mill not far off to get some meal. When she reached the mill she found that it would be some time before she could get some, and it was getting late when she started on her homeward journey. As she walked along under her burden feeling so thankful that they would now have bread, and that she would reach anxious little ones by night, but as she walked wearily along, with these thoughts, she saw some men away down the road before her. What can that mean she thought, and continued on. In getting nearer she saw some horses, and when nearer she saw that the men had on blue uniforms. Oh! they are Union soldiers, but surely they will let a woman like me and in my condition pass when I tell them all about it, she thought.

She was now more anxious to reach home than before. As she

came up to where the men were, one man with a gun in hand demanded "halt". She halted and said, "you must let me pass", and then related her circumstances, telling them of her three children. The officer in charge in a very polite manner said, "madam we would be very glad to let you pass and go to your children, but it is strictly against our orders and cannot let you do it," but she pleaded as a woman can for the sake of her children to let her pass, and was again refused. She then turned around and walked back, with a sad and burdened heart to try and make the best of it she could. After going back some distance she retired to a lonely place and there lifted her heart and hands towards heaven and offered up such a prayer as only women can offer in behalf of their children that they would be spared.

The children were now anxiously waiting her return. They had heard cannonading nearer than before and could hear men at a distance, but did not know the meaning of it. Dark came on and no mother had returned. Perhaps finally they went to sleep and passed the night in sad dreams. Early the next morning they were awakened by hearing heavy cannonading not far off, finally they could hear small arms, and the sound got nearer and nearer, and balls began to strike the house; they got in one corner of the house not knowing what else to do, presently they heard something roaring outside and looked out to see what the trouble was and saw great flames of fire coming through the forest and approaching the house; they rushed for the door and opened it and made their escape, just in time to save themselves, making their way the best they could through the smoke, shells, and balls until they were received by some Confederate soldiers, and were conveyed safely to the rear. To make this incident short, the mother received her children.

It continued to rain and everything was in a bad condition. We now broke our line of battle, and started one evening for our old camps near Fredericksburg, a distance of about fifteen miles. Night came on and it was dark and dreary, some reached camp sometime that night, and many did not get there until next day. We were foot-sore, some barefooted, clothes badly soiled, very despondent, but feeling very thankful that we were spared and back to our old camp once more, for there were so many of our comrades that left when we did that would never return.

We again commenced picket work on the Rappahannock River, drilling and recruiting the broken ranks. We had clothes and shoes furnished us, and began to be ourselves again. As I have said before Rev. A. D. Betts was our Chaplain. He and other Chaplains now began to do some very earnest work among the soldiers. The weather was pleasant and men began to think more about their spiritual condition, perhaps than they had before, as they were beginning to see more of the evils of war, the certainty of death, and the uncertainty of life. Therefore the Chaplains could begin to get their attention to their preaching. Many professed faith in Christ and were baptized.[23]

I remember one morning as Chaplain Betts held a prayer meeting, as he called it, in the sunshine, in the corner of a field, and made some very earnest remarks to the soldiers in regard to their spiritual condition, and then gave an invitation to any that had then trusted to come forward and manifest it; many went forward and claimed a hope in Christ, which I think the most were genuine. Among the many was a young man, a member of the same Company I was, and a man that was very wicked; it seemed that there had been nothing that had been too bad for him to do, he now came forward and claimed a hope which we believe was genuine. He seemed to be altogether a different man afterwards, and was killed in a few months, claiming just before life left him that his hopes were bright for eternity.[24]

General Lee was now having his army equipped the best he could and preparing for the Pennsylvania Campaign. He had a general review which showed up well and that his army was in good condition. With the bright hopes for the Confederacy that was before us now, and General Lee knowing that something would have to be done soon, about the first of June we broke camp near Fredericksburg, the place where we had passed so many cold, chilly and almost sleepless nights on the outpost and elsewhere. The winter had been very burdensome, yet we had enjoyed privileges, and had enjoyed having the gospel preached to us, so we were somewhat loathe to leave the place, but were now on our way to Pennsylvania. Yes, many, oh, many, never to return, but we were in good spirits.

We were to make our way to Culpeper C. H. In a few days we reached Brandy Station, a few miles from Orange C. H.[25] When we reached here Stuart's Cavalry had the enemy engaged. We were called into action and the enemy fled. Night came on, and we struck camp for the night. I was called out on duty after a hard day's march, but spent the night very well. The next morning I did not do very well, but was able to attend to my duty. We did not move until the evening after the morning. I was taken with a chill, and then a fever, and by twelve o'clock I was so sick that I could not sit up. The army was now about ready to move. They were now on their way to the memorable battle of Gettysburg. We now separated for some time. I will now tell about myself, as I am mostly writing my own record.

Notes

1 Hooker: Joseph Hooker (1814–1879) took command of the Army of the Potomac in January 1863.   **Chancellorsville:** The Battle of Chancellorsville was fought April 30–May 6, 1863. Chancellorsville was the designation of a crossroads with an inn about twelve miles from Fredericksburg. The campaign began not on May 1 but several days earlier, with Hooker's crossing of the Rappahannock River on April 27 and the Rapidan River on the 30th.

2 See page 31, note 9 on sharpshooters.

3 May 2: It was actually May 1.

4 a flank move: On May 2, Jackson marched his army to his left and through a forest, around the right wing of the unsuspecting Union forces commanded by General Oliver O. Howard. The surprise attack from a wholly unexpected direction caused a Union rout.

5 fifteen or twenty: In fact, about twelve miles.

6 'Johnnie Rebel': Johnny Rebel and Johnny Reb were slang names for Confederates used by Union soldiers.

7 a few days: Jackson's left arm was amputated May 2. After a twenty-seven-mile ambulance trip, he died of pneumonia on May 10.

8 Godly man: The implication is that sufficient religious zeal, more than military prowess or resources, could have brought success to the cause, and the clear corollary is that weak faith might have been the cause of defeat. JWB attributes this view to others, stopping short of endorsing it. For those like Parker who were convinced that the Confederate cause could not fail because it was God's own, the failure of the war was a spiritual as much as a military and political shock. How could God let this happen? It "forced Christians in that region," writes Kent Dollar, "to reconcile their faith with the defeat of the Confederacy....Although tens of thousands of Confederates had become God-fearing soldiers during the war, Christians maintained that the South as a whole had turned away from the Lord." Kent T. Dollar, "'Strangers in a Strange Land': Christian Soldiers in the Early Months of the Civil War"; Sheehan-Dean, 165.

9 Pegram's battery: William R. Pegram (1841–1865) commanded an artillery battalion with a battery placed near Hazel Grove, west of Chancellorsville crossroads and south of the Orange Turnpike, now Route 3.

10 getting near: When the 30th got near, the enemy retreated, and the Confederates used their opportunity.

11 foreigners: The house was at the intersection of the east-west Orange Turnpike and the north-south Orange Plank Road (Route 610). The foundation remains.

12 control over the fire: It is not clear how soldiers carrying muskets and cartridge boxes were equipped to put out a forest fire, but possibly it was mainly in low brush and they were able to beat it down, perhaps with entrenching tools.

13 on the field: The 30th suffered thirty-seven killed or mortally wounded, seventy-five others wounded. Company I lost seven killed or mortally wounded (Taylor, 428, 430).

14 they would be dead: Such realized premonitions were common. "Many letters announcing the deaths of comrades commented on the deceased's foreboding that a particular encounter would indeed prove fatal," writes Faust. "On the night before his last battle in Virginia in 1862, Willie Bacon had told his comrades of his conviction he would die. 'Strange and mysterious,' remarked the preacher who delivered his funeral sermon, 'is the fact that God so often permits the shadow of death to be thrown upon us, that we may prepare ourselves for his coming'" (Faust 2008, 19). The behavior of JWB's comrade seems almost suicidal, as though he would rather die than endure any longer the mental strain of combat.

15 Stuart: James Ewell Brown "Jeb" Stuart (1833–1864) commanded a cavalry brigade that accompanied Jackson on the flanking march on May 2. After Jackson and Major General A. P. Hill were wounded, Stuart took command of the Second Corps at Chancellorsville on May 3.

16 morning dawned: May 5

17 knocked it from his body: One of very few grisly details in the memoir. Even so, JWB makes the effect of a cannonball on the human head seem almost mild, like a pumpkin pushed off a post.

18 The next night: Hooker and his defeated army recrossed the Rappahannock on May 6.

19 Hooker having: Hooker had about 130,000 men, while Lee had about 60,000.

20 great loss: Confederate losses in killed and wounded were more than 12,000, while Union losses exceeded 17,000.

21 were gone: Victory by the army is little consolation for personal loss.

22 the gum: "chiefly Midland [i.e., Midwest and upper South]: a vessel or container made of a hollow log." *Webster's Third New International Dictionary* (Springfield, Mass.: Merriam-Webster, 1993).

23 baptized: With its unexpected terrors and unprecedented scale of death, the war sparked an explosion of religious intensity on both sides. In the Confederate armies, from a region with a revivalist tradition, the effect was stronger. "In the fall of 1862, religious revivals broke out in the Army of Northern Virginia, followed by others in the Army of Tennessee and in the Union armies, initiating a wave of revivalism that lasted for the remainder of the war. Chaplains, missionaries, and local ministers preached to eager audiences, and tens of thousands of fighting men experienced conversion" (Dollar, 160). Faust writes, "When the timing of battle permitted, chaplains and lay preachers organized a prodigious schedule of services — sometimes as many as five or six meetings a day. During a six-week lull in the fighting in Virginia during the summer of 1864 — a time when the military situation made invocation of divine help particularly appropriate — one brigade chaplain scheduled daily prayers at sunrise, an 'inquiry meeting' each morning at eight, preaching at eleven, prayers for the success of the Confederate cause at four, and preaching again at night." Faust, "Christian Soldiers: The Meaning of Revivalism in the Confederate Army," *Journal of Southern History* 53, no. 1 (February 1987): 63–90, cited in Barton and Logue, 327–8. The mingling of fighting and religion is described in Chaplain Betts's diary for 1864: "August 12 — Move and camp two miles N. W. of Strasburg. August 13 —

Troops in line of battle. Sunday, August 14 — Quiet. Bro. Power preaches in a. m. and I preach in p. m. Prayer meeting at night. August 16 — Preach to Hoke's Brigade in a. m. and to Johnston's in p. m. Prayer meeting at night. August 17 — Our men drive the enemy from W. Mills" (Betts, 64).

24 bright for eternity: The soldier converts and then is killed, but his conversion gives him serenity. The nature of his wickedness is unclear but does not sound criminal. As with Singleton Langley, the soldier's positive attitude toward his fate is reported.

25 Brandy Station: The Battle of Brandy Station, June 9, 1863, was the largest cavalry battle of the war. General J. E. B. Stuart threw back a surprise Union attack, but his losses were heavy.

5.

SICKNESS

June 1863–May 1864

At this time my condition was a sad one. I had to separate with comrades and friends, many forever, and I was now thrown entirely among strangers and very sick. A severe attack of brain fever had taken hold of me.[1] I was now put on an ambulance, and the army started one way, and I was taken the other which was a very sad thing to me at this time. My fever was getting very high and I was unable to stand and had to be carried to the ambulance. The distance from Orange C. H. to the nearest station where the train could be reached I suppose was about ten miles. I did not have much more recollection about anything until we reached the C. H. I now recollect being taken from the ambulance, fainted and had some water poured on me to revive me. I was left here, where or how long I do not know, but I was put on the train and the next thing I remember was being taken from the train.

I found out later that I was at Gordonsville, Virginia, a distance from where I left of about fifteen miles.[2] I was now carried to a ward in the hospital that was scarcely occupied by anybody. I passed the remainder of the night very restless, without any attention. The next morning nobody seemed to give me any attention. After awhile there came a man to me and said, "if you want any breakfast, you go down to the dining room and get some." I told him that I did not want any, but wanted a doctor to come and see me, and he said, "one will come after awhile," and then he left. My fever was not so high now, but I was getting very restless.[3] Sometime that evening a person came to me, and I suppose it was the wardmaster, and I told him that I wanted something done. A little later I was taken and carried over to another ward, and here I was given some clothes and began to be noticed a little, but continued to get worse, fortunately for me one of the best doctors of the medical board attended that ward, and he would call in other doctors to pass their judgment upon my case.[4]

It was now sometime in June and the weather was very hot, and I with a high fever altogether in my head. The doctor kept me as full of quinine as I could bear.[5] The ward had some thirty or forty inmates and several bad cases.[6] One corner of the ward was used as a dead corner, (as the nurses called it).[7] When one was almost dead they would place him in that corner, so that others would not see much of him. When I was carried in, I was placed in that corner, the one in there soon died, the next worse case was put in, and in a few days he died; it was thought that I would be the next one, so I was put in, but I lived until it was seen that I had taken a change for better, and then I was moved somewhere else.

I will say here that I think my recovery was due to a great extent to having ice beat in small pieces, and applied to my forehead. I got so weak that I remember fainting many times, when I would be moved about, but I was attended to very well, considering only men waited on me. It seemed that if a woman had walked through the room so that I could have seen her that it would have done me good.[8] After awhile I took a turn for better, but I was still very low down, and it took me sometime to get back to myself again.[9]

Sometime about the last of July, it was thought that I was able to go home, so I was given my furlough and sent off. I reached home very much jaded; it being sixteen months since I last left there. I remained here until sometime in October, but when I felt sufficiently able to try army life again I left for my command; it then being near where I was taken sick, having a great many doubts of about whether I would ever return.

I made my way to Gordonsville, the place where I was furloughed from. I was stopped here with several hundred more, as the main army was then moving and had a small fight at Bristow Station. As soon as the army got settled we were told to go to our commands. I reached my command down on the Rappahannock River. They had been in two fights since I left them, Gettysburg and Bristow Station, but had not lost many men by death; the company that I belonged to had greatly recruited and numbered a great many.[10] In a short time, the regiment was ordered on picket duty at Kelly's Ford on the Rappahannock River.[11] Here the army placed some artillery on an elevated place on the other side where they had a great advantage over our men.[12] The 50th Regiment was on picket duty at the Ford, and they opened their artillery down on us, with grape shot and canister shell, then sending a strong line of infantry down to the Ford and opening fire at our side where we had but little protection. Our men were compelled to give way and surrender, but something had to be done and done soon.

Col. Sillers was in command of the Regiment (a good Colonel). He gave orders to fall back. The enemy's fire was very heavy, and there was such an elevated slope to ascend from, many did not try it, and were captured there. Several made their escape through shells and bullets. A good many of the regiment was killed and wounded.[13] Colonel Sillers was killed. The Company that I was a member of had one-half of them killed, wounded and captured, scarcely any that were captured ever returned to the Regiment, as the North would not exchange but few prisoners, and most of them remained in prison until the close of the war. This was one way the North managed to beat the South. We held theirs, but they had plenty more at their command, and we did not.[14]

The enemy crossed the river, and we continued to fall back, keeping the railroad guarded, and to be sure we kept ourselves the best we could between them and Richmond; this was sometime in

November. We camped and did picket duty along down the river towards Fredericksburg, not staying at one place long at the time. About the first of December, the enemy put their army across the river and made a stand.[15] We were down the river, but made our way there.

I remember one night while we were on the way that we got so near on the enemy that we were commanded in a whisper from one another down the line that if we were fired on, not to return the fire, but to lay down. The weather was very bad at this time, it was very cold, rained, hailed, and snowed, and could not have much fire, so we suffered very much. We fortified ourselves and there was much cannonading, and the sharpshooters skirmished very heavy, and a few slight engagements were made, but they for some reason withdrew their army back across the river. The night they recrossed was a dark, rainy one, fairing off just before day, and turning very windy and cold.

At this time I contracted a deep cold and that morning was taken with a pain in my lungs, which resulted in pneumonia; the army was now beginning to move.[16] I was not able to go, so I was left by the side of the road, with a comrade with me to get me on an ambulance and have me carried to the railroad but there was no ambulance to be found. Now my condition was very serious. Here, I lay beside the road on some boards to keep me off the damp ground. My comrade covered me with a blanket and built a fire near. The pneumonia took deep hold on me; my comrades all gone but one, I not able to travel and a distance of twenty-five miles from a railroad. The country around being a part of that known as the Wilderness, most of the inhabitants had moved out, and the armies had raided through time and again.[17] While this was my condition the cold December winds blew very rapid at times. The weather continued to get colder, and here we remained thinking there was some hope, but as the evening began to draw nearer, I could see that my companion was getting restless, and in our condition we had something to get serious about, but later providence turned for us (it must have been).

Late that evening there came along a soldier from some hospital on his way to his command, and stopped where we were. On being told who I was and where I was from, he said he knew my uncle of Wilson county, and that he would stop and stay with us during the night, as he had to camp somewhere beside the road.[18] He told us that there was a house just up the road, so my companion went off to look for it, and soon came back telling us that there was a house there that was not occupied. The inhabitants had left it, so they managed to get me to it, I being very sick. After we reached there, they made a good fire in one of the fireplaces, and laid me down on the floor before it. Our hope of getting any assistance in getting me away seemed very gloomy, as the army had gone on somewhere, and we were left here in this desolate country, but providence continued to provide. Sometime that night after dark there rode some men up to the house for a place to spend the night from the cold winds. It was a General and staff. I think it was General Stuart. On taking in the situation they asked my comrades to move me in the other room which was smaller and let them occupy the larger which they did. There was a fireplace in the smaller room. There was a doctor with them and he gave me some medicine, that being the first treatment that I had gotten. We passed through the night the best we could, I being a little restless. The next morning the General and doctor had me put on their ambulance and carried to Orange C. H., a distance I think of twenty-five miles. It took us nearly all day to get there, this being the first time I had been here since I was there last with the brain fever. I spent the night in the hospital and had very little attention.[19] The next day I was carried on the train to Charlottesville, Virginia, reaching there late that evening.[20] I was carried to a three story brick hospital and was taken to a room on the third floor.[21]

Three days had passed by and I was getting very sick. I began to get some treatment for my case, but I had quite a hard time and it was some time before I got well. There were two ladies that superintended this hospital and they would make one or two rounds a day, and see that things were attended to and kept in proper shape.[22] I gradually improved and the wardmaster took me to assist him. I spent the winter here and had a very pleasant time, as they would let me go down town at any time and go to the State University which was very interesting.[23] I was also allowed to go to preaching and Sunday school.

It was in March when orders were sent out for all able bodied men to report to their commands. I was notified to be ready to leave at most any hour; and it was very cold, the ground being covered with snow, but that made no difference. After making many good friends and having good quarters, I was very sad to know that I was again to be thrown out into the cold; but this was nothing for war times.

I was stopped at Gordonsville and sent out with many others to the camp for twenty days to see if smallpox would break out on us. This dreadful disease was raging in most of the hospitals, there being a few cases in the hospital I had just left.[24] One case broke out in the building I was in. It was very unpleasant here, as we were not provided for, and there were men from all parts of the South. I remained here twenty days, nothing of importance occurring. I had my overcoat stolen from me by a South Carolinian, but succeeded in getting it before he disposed of it. I was now sent to my command about ten miles below Orange C. H. I found my command in very good quarters, and everything was very quiet. Up to this time the regiment was doing picket duty occasionally down the Rappahannock River.

A few days passed and the Regiment was ordered about five miles from camp on picket duty. It snowed nearly one foot deep, and we were down beside the river with no protection. The only thing do to was to tough it out.

At another time, I was put in charge of a squad of men and

placed near a ford to guard it, and remained there nearly a week before we were relieved.[25] We were very well clothed at this time. Some of the men went into something for amusement, and a Lee Brigade built them a theater, and acted once a week.[26] The Chaplains had chapels built and had very good services. Many professed faith in Christ. It was said that a certain Company from Nash County had sixteen men to make profession and that they all got killed before the following campaign was over. It seemed that it was often the case that the men who claimed a hope would be killed and the sinner spared longer to have another opportunity for repentance.[27] We were here until May. They would let us sleep until sunrise in the morning. Every preparation was made that could be for the coming campaign, and we looked forward to it with a solemn dread, for we were certain it was coming, and not long off.

Notes

1 brain fever: A generic nineteenth-century term for any kind of severe brain inflammation, commonly viral encephalitis or viral meningitis. The former is often transmitted by a mosquito bite.

2 fifteen miles: In March 1862, the Exchange Hotel in Gordonsville, a key rail junction of the Orange and Alexandria and Virginia Central railroads, was converted to the Gordonsville Receiving Hospital, which treated approximately 70,000 men in the course of the war. The hospital admitted 23,642 patients in a single year between June 1, 1863, and May 5, 1864. Today it is a museum. The hospital's admission records, preserved at the Museum of the Confederacy in Richmond (OS Box 3, General Hospital Gordonsville, No. 3474, p. 71), indicate that "John Bowen" was admitted June 12 with "Int. feb.," an abbreviation for febris intermittens, that is, malaria. For "febris intermittens," see Jack D. Welch, *Two Confederate Hospitals and Their Patients: Atlanta to Opelika* (Macon: Mercer University Press, 2005), 100. Other causes for soldiers' admission listed in the same Gordonsville record book include diarrhea, bronchitis, "debilitita" (i.e., severe debilitation), typhoid, piles, dysentery, scurvy, gonorrhea, pleurisy, and erysipelas — a painful skin infection. The leading cause of death by disease was intestinal infection: typhoid, diarrhea, or dysentery.

3 very restless: In malaria, fever rises and falls in forty-eight-to-seventy-two-hour cycles.

4 medical board: An independent board of examiners authorized to review cases and grant furloughs or medical discharges. Regimental surgeons were not so empowered, since they might be subject to personal favoritism.

5 quinine: An antimalarial medication made from the bark of the cinchona tree. It was for centuries the only remedy for the disease and is still in use. JWB was fortunate to be in relatively capable hands. While many surgeons were well trained by the best standards of the time, there were few first-rate medical schools in the South, and unregulated diploma mills turned out "doctors" at a high rate. In the antebellum decades, writes Cunningham, "the standards in medical education, instead of being raised, were sinking" (Cunningham, 14–15).

6 thirty or forty: The rooms in the Exchange Hotel are too small to accommodate forty men, which suggests that JWB was in one of the numerous separate buildings or pavilion tents (sheltering about thirty men) used at the complex.

7 a dead corner: The system of segregating hopeless cases while attending to other patients would later be called triage.

8 a woman: It is not clear why JWB thinks he would have done better if a woman had walked in; perhaps he simply means that a warm feminine touch would have had a healing effect, or that she would stand in place of a female loved one. See also Faust (2008, 12) for Clara Barton's famous kiss of a dying delirious Union soldier, who supposed that she was his sister. Early in the war, there was strong opposition to women as nurses. One Northern physician wrote, "Imagine a delicate refined woman assisting a rough soldier to the closet-stool, or supplying him with a bedpan, or adjusting the knots on a T-bandage employed in retaining a urinary catheter in position. . . . Women, in my humble opinion, are utterly and decidedly unfit for such service" (Rutkow, 170). However, opposition weakened as the need grew. The most famous Confederate woman nurse was Phoebe Pember (1823–1913), from a prominent South Carolina Jewish family, who served as matron at Chimborazo Hospital and published her memoirs in 1879. See Phoebe Yates Pember, *A Southern Woman's Story* (Whitefish, Mont.: Kessinger Publishing, 2010). Roman Catholic nuns, especially the Sisters of Charity, nursed the wounded of both sides with such effectiveness that administrators and field surgeons welcomed them gratefully (Rutkow, 168–9). Partly as a result of Civil War service, nursing became the first acceptable professional work for women.

9 back to myself again: His recovery from this and other illnesses, to say nothing of wounds, must be partly attributed to an extraordinary constitution and immune system. Ira Rutkow reports that malaria was "long endemic and epidemic in Washington and points south . . . the second most common camp-related disease" — the first was intestinal diseases such as typhoid and dysentery. "Northern medical records detail almost 1.4 million cases with more than 15,000 deaths during the forty-eight months of conflict. Incomplete Confederate records for 1861 and 1862 total 165,000 cases and more than 1,300 deaths" (Rutkow, 15). JWB's youth also worked in his favor. "The immense hardships of military life," Glatthaar writes, "broke down older soldiers, reducing their resistance to disease. Although younger men did not care for themselves as well and probably had less exposure to killing illnesses in their youthful lives, they generally had stronger constitutions and could fight off sickness better than their older comrades-in-arms." The death rate from disease of soldiers under age twenty was about 7 percent (Glatthaar, 18).

10 Gettysburg and Bristow Station: The Battle of Gettysburg, in Pennsylvania, was fought July 1–3, 1863. The 30th Regiment started with about 278 men and suffered seventy killed, missing, wounded, or captured. Parker was severely wounded in the face and did not return to service for six months. Lieutenant Colonel William W. Sillers (a graduate of Harvard's Lawrence Scientific School) succeeded him. The regiment returned to Orange Court House on August 8, after a journey of 180 miles over thirty days. The Battle of Bristoe Station, October 14, 1863, was a Confederate defeat that tarnished the reputation of General A. P. Hill.

11 Kelly's Ford: This was the second fight at this location — about thirty-five miles north of Gordonsville — on November 7, 1863, sometimes called the Second Battle of Rappahannock Station. The better-known Battle of Kelly's Ford took place the previous March 17.

12 the army: A possible transcription error. More likely "the enemy."

13 killed and wounded: The 30th Regiment suffering 181 casualties, the heaviest of any battle during the war.

14 we did not: At the beginning of the war, the United States would not exchange prisoners on grounds that to do so would recognize the standing of the Confederacy. In July 1862, Confederate general D. H. Hill and Union major general John A. Dix concluded an agreement for the general exchange of prisoners, known as the Dix-Hill Cartel. However, General Ulysses S. Grant stopped exchanges after he took command in March 1864, knowing that the Union army could replace its captured men, but the Confederates could not.

15 first of December: The 30th Regiment camped near Morton's Ford on the Rapidan River. Between November 27 and December 3, it engaged in minor skirmishes. The regiment remained here until the beginning of the Wilderness Campaign in May 1864.

16 pneumonia: The fifth serious illness again separates him from the command. Luckily, this time he has a loyal comrade — as usual, unidentified — to help him.

17 the Wilderness: An area in northern Spotsylvania County along the Rapidan River.

18 Wilson county: JWB had three uncles: William, Calvin, and John Bone. Family records give no evidence of which uncle was living outside Nash County. Wilson County adjoins Nash to the south.

19 the hospital: This seems to be once again the Gordonsville Receiving Hospital, since that is where he was admitted with malaria ("brain fever") the previous June, sent via rail by way of Orange. There had been an army hospital in Orange, but it closed in 1862.

20 Charlottesville: About twenty miles southwest of Gordonsville.

21 three story brick hospital: JWB's service record shows that he was admitted to C.S.A General Hospital, Charlottesville, with "pleuritis" — that is, pleurisy — on December 4 and discharged for return to duty February 16, 1864. Pleurisy is a severely painful inflammation of the pleura, the outer lining of the lung. The hospital had 500 beds at its peak and admitted 22,700 patients during the war.

22 two ladies: The identity of the women is unknown; however, the Charlottesville hospital did have women officials. For a time in 1861 it had employed Oriana Moon Andrews, one of the few female surgeons in the United States, and apparently the only one in the Confederate medical service, as director of nursing. See Lisa Tendrich Frank, *Women in the American Civil War,* vol. 1 (Santa Barbara: ABC-CLIO Inc., 2008), 103.

23 State University: The University of Virginia. It is not clear what is meant by "go to" the university, whether he was allowed to sit in on classes or in some other way interact with students or faculty. The university, at the time the largest in the South, remained open throughout the war.

24 disease: Nearly three years into the war, epidemics are still "raging." Gordonsville had a smallpox quarantine area to the east of the main hospital. At Chimborazo, and probably also Gordonsville, all patients were vaccinated before discharge. Malaria especially, since infection did not confer immunity, remained a stubborn killer (Rutkow, 15).

25 put in charge of a squad: A squad is about ten men, normally commanded by a corporal. Later (see p. 74) he describes twelve under his command. He mentions no promotion, however, and his service record lists him as a private at war's end. It appears to be a temporary ad hoc assignment.

26 Lee Brigade: The meaning of "Lee Brigade" is unclear; JWB might have used the term to indicate that the theater was not built by his regiment. F. M. Parker wrote to his wife in March 1864, "The army is in the best spirits . . . we have every thing to cheer us up at this time" (Taylor, 317–18). When in camp for long periods, soldiers invented diversions to prevent boredom. Games, music, and theatricals helped pass the time.

27 sinners spared: Like many others affected by the war, most famously Lincoln in his Second Inaugural Address ("Both [sides] read the same Bible, and pray to the same God; and each invokes His aid against the other. . . . The prayers of both could not be answered; that of neither has been answered fully"), JWB tries to fathom the intentions of the Almighty. If what he says were widely believed, that accepting Christ makes one more likely to be killed, one would expect more men to have hesitated to convert. It is clear to John Wesley, at least, that God is carefully making decisions in individual cases, and that one's response to ministerial importuning might make all the difference. Hence a particular camp religious service can have implications as fateful as those of a battle, and the war becomes a stage in the larger drama of salvation.

6.

SPOTSYLVANIA COURT HOUSE

May–July 1864

On Monday morning, May 3rd, we broke camp at a place where we had had much pastime, where there had been many an earnest prayer offered, and a place where many, oh many of us would never see anymore. With these serious reflections we left and went down to the picket line, and took our place on the bank of the river, while the enemy occupied the other side. We remained quiet that day and the next, but on Tuesday night, the enemy commenced crossing the river below us. I was now in command of a part, and was ordered to take my men, and leave sometime betwixt midnight and day. The rest of the regiment left after we were some distance away, and we were then ordered back to our same post. We remained there until sometime that evening, and we were then ordered to leave again. They were now fighting below us; this was Wednesday, May 5th.

The great campaign of 1864 had now opened, with the battle of the Wilderness.[1] We went forward, but were not engaged in battle that day or night. Early next morning we went forward to where some of the army was fighting, and formed line of battle. We then made temporary breastworks, but the enemy did not attack us. In the evening we attacked them by flank move, routing and driving them back with some loss to both sides, and we again made breastworks and held our position for the next two days.[2] On Saturday the enemy commenced moving their army from the Wilderness to Spotsylvania Court House some distance below.[3] The next day I remember that we had orders read to us that the enemy had reached Spotsylvania and had been repulsed.

On the ninth day of May, a very, very warm day for this time of year, we were notified that we were needed, and a heavy penalty would be placed upon us, if we did not report to duty. We started and made quick time, stopping a few minutes in every two hours. Many men threw most of their baggage away, only keeping their guns, cartridge boxes and canteens. Some of the best soldiers had to give up owing to the hot weather, and were left beside the road. We reached the place in the evening and formed line of battle, and advanced forward. We did not go far before we were upon the enemy. We fought and drove them back until night came on. In this attack my left hand comrade was again wounded. The orderly Sergeants of three different Companies were killed, and many were wounded, while others were taken as prisoners.

We now got a location and made breastworks that night, and held this position for the next two days, expecting to be attacked at any time. The sharpshooters kept up a fire on us the entire night, the picket line not being very far off. I remember during these nights that the sharpshooters would fire so heavily at times that we would be certain of an attack, and would arouse from our slumber to our muskets. We rose at times in our slumbers and would get at place with our muskets, and orders were given. The alarm was given so often during the night that we got very familiar with it. Fighting was going on both our left and right. On the left the enemy attacked our line of battle in our breastworks several times, but were not successful in taking us.[4] As soon as they had fallen back our men mounted their works and got their guns and ammunition, and brought them over to our side.

In the next attack we were more prepared, and drove their lines back three times, with heavy loss to their side and a very small loss to ours. This was a very bad position, as the men stood in danger of being wounded or hit by the enemy, but much to our surprise we found that the trouble was caused by a man up in a tree who was shooting in our midst. We finally located the tree, and commenced firing at it, but by some means the marksman disappeared. Our breastwork on our right was made in a curve, and called in History the "Horse Shoe," owing to its shape. It was built in this way to get the location for the artillery, and was nearly one mile in length and not quite one-half mile at the base.[5]

Ramseur's Brigade was moved towards the right on the night of the eleventh, and placed in position.[6] There was an attack expected somewhere that night from the movements of the enemy, but we were not certain at what place, but we were all on the lookout. I was put in charge of twelve men, and ordered to post them on the works in front of our Company, and relieve them every two hours, this I did until midnight, and then I was relieved. We had a heavy rain most of the night, which kept me from getting very much sleep.

The next morning was very damp; this was Tuesday, and memorable, the twelfth of May. About sunrise the enemy massed their troops in front of the Horse Shoe, and attacked and drove the men out.[7] The enemy now held both lines of the works, and moved some of our artillery; this left them in a position to shell right and left along our lines, and they did not fail to use their opportunity, almost taking our works.[8] We then realized that we must take the Horse Shoe back for we could not stay in this position much longer. The commanding officer decided to take the works back.[9] General Ramseur was ordered to take his Brigade and charge the works. We were now taken in front of the shoe, and formed in line of battle.[10]

While this was being done, the enemy was firing their shells and grape shot into our lines. We were exposed very much while forming line of battle. Many were wounded at this point. I remember hearing General Ramseur say to Colonel Parker, "Colonel we have got to charge those works, and get them back," and he

The Army of the Potomac: A Sharp-Shooter on Picket Duty,
Winslow Homer. The sniper is equipped with a specialized
rifle with a telescopic sight.
(Harper's Weekly, November 15, 1862)

answered, "We can do it." This was a serious time with us, and
would have been more so, if we could really realize our position.
Here we were, one line of men, with two ranks (front and rear),
and in front of us were two lines of breastworks, filled with men
and artillery placed at convenient points.[11]

We now moved forward and many, oh many, made their last
charge here. This field was the last resting place of many good soldiers, and came very near being one for the writer. We now passed
the sharpshooters, and men were being wounded all along the line.
We had orders to charge, and charge we did. Just before we reached
the first line of works, I was mortally wounded by a ball striking
me in the right breast passing through my lungs and coming out
beside my backbone, and lodging in some clothes that I had on my
back.[12] (I now have the ball.)[13] I realized that I was wounded, but

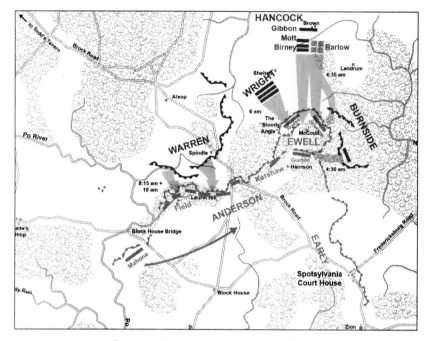

The order of battle, May 12, 1864, in the Mule Shoe, Battle of
Spotsylvania Court House. The partial inner line of entrenchments
("the first line of works") shows to the right of "Rodes."
(Map by Hal Jespersen, www.cwmaps.com)

did not know how bad. I got my knife out and cut my cartridge
box from me; by this time I was very sick, and every breath seemed
to get shorter and the pain increased. I began to think I was going
to die. I soon gained a little strength and took a little encouragement. I realized that our men had carried the works, but the fighting continued, and did not seem but a short distance away, as the
balls were striking around me from what I learned later.[14]

At this point our men were trying to take the second line of
works, and did succeed, but had it hand to hand in some places.
I decided that our men were having a very hard time, and probably would not succeed, and would have to fall back. I thought if I

The minié ball that pierced John Wesley's chest.
(Family collection)

could get back I had better do it, so I got up, but did not go but a
short distance before I had to give up from weakness; here another
ball struck me. I revived a little and started again, but soon had
to give up. I now had a little hill to ascend, and as I was on my
way another ball struck me.[15] I saw a cherry tree on the top of the
hill, and made my way to it. I managed to get to the tree and laid
down, as I was very weak from the loss of so much blood.

The battle was still raging, and the balls and shells were striking
around me, but did not hit me as the tree was two feet thick at the
ground. I did not stop here very long before I attempted to go further, but found that I was unable to do so, and too I thought the litter bearers would come and get the wounded up. My clothes were all
wet from the rain that had fallen the night before, and as I had not
eaten anything since the day before or gotten very much sleep, I was
in bad circumstances and getting worse. The battle continued on,
and no one came near me. Our men had taken both lines of works,
but the enemy was fortified, and the lines were so near together that
there was a heavy fire kept up by musket and cannon all day, and the
enemy had located themselves so that they had a cross fire on a part

of the works, and killed many of our men during the day. Captain Harris and my nearest comrade were both killed.

There was an oak tree nearly twenty inches through standing near the works, and was shot down by the balls. (The trunk is now in the museum at Washington City.)[16] The day was far spent, and a shell from a cannon struck the ground, and continued to bounce in my direction, but stopped just before it hit me. Night was coming on with no prospect of help. I unrolled my blanket and tried to spread it over me the best I could. I was on wet ground, hungry, sleepy, weak and bloody; this was my condition for the night, the fighting still going on. I slumbered, at times, through the night, and would find myself calling some of the litter bearers for water. I could hear others that were wounded doing the same thing, but no relief came. Our men fell back during the night, and formed a line of battle on the other side of me.[17]

The next morning was damp, misty and smoky. Everything was very quiet, and seemed like a dream to me. Finally, my attention was aroused by hearing someone coming up to me, on looking I saw one of our soldiers, and he laid down some knapsacks that he had picked up from the fields, and was going to search them. I asked him his command. I then wanted to know if he would give me a drink of water, which he did by pouring some in my canteen. I don't know how much. While he was doing this I asked him where our army was, for I was certain that they had moved in some direction. At this moment I heard a sharp report from a rifle. My companion gave me a short answer. I did not know what he said, for he was of French descent and jumped up and ran leaving his plunder where he had laid it.[18] I could now see others running from the field, this caused me to try to look that way.[19] When I did I saw a picket line of blue coats coming; they halted and formed a line of battle in about one hundred yards of me, and commenced firing on our men. None can scarcely imagine my feelings when I found out they were so near to me. My location was in view of

Hancock's Corps Assaulting the Works at the "Bloody Angle,"
by William Brooke Thomas Trego, 1887.
(Matt Flynn photo, courtesy of Cooper Hewitt, Smithsonian Design Museum)

both lines. I had first feared that the enemy would get me; but I now saw that they could not.

This was Friday morning, May 13th. It continued to rain in small showers all through the day. I continued to slumber at times, but would be aroused very often by the sharp report of the enemy's guns. During the day I pulled the haversack to me that my comrade had left and searched it to see if it contained something to eat, but found nothing that I wanted, but tried to eat some soda crackers and sugar; this being about the first thing that I had eaten since I had been wounded. Water was what I wanted. I found a large cup in the sack, and took it and put it down near me, and as the showers would fall a little water would fall into the cup and water would drop off the leaves of the tree, and in this way I got a little water.[20] The day passed away, each line held their position. The night came on, the cries of the wounded would be heard all through the night.

Now and then the pickets on each side would fire at each other. I passed through the night very restless.

Morning again came, things seemed about like they were the day before.[21] The weather cleared a little, but was still cloudy. I slumbered a little all through the day and was very weak, but gaining my nerve a little. Evening came on, and it seemed that the enemy was going to make an attack upon our line. The sharpshooters commenced firing more regularly. There was a very good dwelling located about seventy-five yards from me, and it was also near the enemy's picket line. Some of their men were in it, and they were shooting from the windows and other places.[22] I could lie and see what they were doing. They moved a battery near their line and opened fire on us. I could hear them give the command to load and fire. Seeing and hearing all of this and making no attack upon us I decided they were making arrangements to make an attack the next day.

As I have said before, my nerve was getting to be stronger. It was reasonable that there would be another fight right over where I was, which side would gain was uncertain, or I might be killed, or our men could fall back and the enemy could get me, and if they did it would very likely mean death for me. I was certain that I could not remain as I now was much longer without having my wound attended to, and without food and water. This being the case I thought this would be my last resting place.

My condition was a sad one, but if I could get to my comrades there was some hope. I did not know how bad I was wounded, considering all these things I began to feel that I could get away if I had an opportunity. Night was coming on, and I began thinking how I could arrange to get away. I could see some cannon redoubts about one hundred and fifty yards from me, and about one hundred yards from our picket line.[23] If I could get to the cannon redoubts during the night it would be as near our line as I dared to go before morning; but getting there was the great trouble. The moon was shining nearly all night, but would go down about one

The McCoull farmhouse within the Mule Shoe,
Spotsylvania Court House, 1861–65.
(Library of Congress)

hour before day.[24] If I went, this would be my only chance when
the pickets could not see me. I now had it planned out, but could I
make it was the question. I had this consolation, I could try and if
I failed my condition probably would not be anymore serious than
it was.

I now turned my thoughts to the Lord, and asked him to help
me and tried to trust him with all my power to help me to get out
from where I was. I again slumbered through the night and was
lying in the right position to see the moon when it would go out of
sight. I tried to get up but had to be very careful. I sat up awhile,
then I reached a stick that laid near me and prized myself up and
started off. I went a short distance but was compelled to stop as I
was very tired, but I made another attempt and succeeded in getting to the cannon redoubts that I had located.

I was now in about one hundred yards of our picket line.

I must now make myself known to our men before it got light enough for the enemy to see me, and I took a white handkerchief from my companion's knapsack and put it on a stick and shook it.[25] I was soon told to come on and I made another start, doubting whether I could reach the line or not, but it was a little down grade, which was to my advantage. Before I reached the line the enemy had located me and then began firing in my direction. I was at the point of falling caused by weakness and pain when an officer at the line came to my assistance and helped me out and laid me down to recover.

No one can realize the relief that I felt in getting delivered to my companions although my condition was critical. Some litter bearers was sent for me and carried me back to an ambulance where the other wounded were; this was Sunday morning. Sometime that day the enemy withdrew their lines and their army commenced moving down the river towards Fredericksburg.[26] It took a good many litter bearers to move the wounded from the field. One of our Regiment was found sitting by a tree with his brains coming out. He died in a few days.

I then received my first treatment. After learning how I was wounded I felt much better although getting out made me much sorer than I was.[27] I found Chaplain Betts here doing all he could for the wounded, and giving many encouraging words for their happiness while departing for eternity. He expressed his good wishes that I had made my escape from death.[28] All the wounded that were able they took to the railroad, so that they could be carried to a hospital for treatment and those that were not they took to a large grove to remain until they improved or died.[29]

Our army was moving on between the enemy and Richmond and it was reasonable that those left would have to remain in this desolate place for sometime. After I had been here two or three days, the leading surgeon came to me one morning and asked me if I thought that I could stand to be carried to the railroad. I being weak and over anxious to get away and did not want to stay in

Union wounded at field hospital, Spotsylvania Court
House, by Mathew Brady.
(National Archives)

this desolate place told him that I thought that I could. He then
told me to be ready to leave in a short time. I asked some of my
comrades to roll up my blankets, they did so and I was ready to go.
Chaplain Betts came around at this time and seeing what was being
done said, "Why Bone, what are you going to do?" I told him. He
said, "Why you cannot stand and don't you go." I told him that I
wanted to be carried but if he thought it best I would not go.

By this time the wagon was ready for me. My way to the railroad was on a heavy four team wagon to be carried about fifteen
miles over a badly worn road, the trip being taken at night and
I would then be left at the station until I could be sent to Richmond.[30] Four men took me on a litter and carried me about two

Rev. A.D. Betts, chaplain of the 30th Regiment, in July 1900.
(Betts family collection)

miles to the place where the wounded were, there being about one thousand of us that were not able to be carried to the railroad.[31] We were a hard looking set of men for we were wounded in almost every way that a man could be to be living. I now realized that my brother Chaplain was right in not letting me be carried to the railroad for I was so sore the next day from the effects of being carried that I could scarcely be moved without pain. I am sure that I would have soon died from the jolt and exposure if I had been put on the wagon and started off the day before.[32] I am very certain that the brother Chaplain was the means of saving my life and I give him credit for same though I did not like it when he opposed to my being carried.[33]

I now wish to take the reader back to the place where I was wounded and try to show the working of the Supreme Power, for I know it was greatly bestowed upon me in my sad condition. I believe, if I had stayed where I was wounded the enemy would have gotten me and in all probability I would have died. If I had gotten off the field and in care of my men in the rush of the wounded I would have been sent to the railroad and as before stated that would have resulted in my death. I was lucky enough to be left just far enough for neither side to get me and I stayed there until the rush was over.[34] I was unable to find out why the man from Louisiana laid down his plunder beside a wounded man and searched it. Everything seemed to be going my way. The moon went down in time for me to make my way out and the cannons were placed in a different direction.[35] I think the man from Louisiana saved my life for he kept me from being sent off.[36] It is a wonder I am living today after going through so much during the war.

We were now given tents to stay in. The wounded died very fast, several would be carried out and buried each day. In the tent I was in three died. One of them being a member of my Company and the other two members of my Regiment. Many a poor fellow would have lived that died if he had only had the proper attention. We had a very tough time. Here we had a doctor or two, and a few men left with us, the latter for cooks and nurses. The Fredericksburg railroad was now cut and our supplies had to be brought in wagons from Orange C. H., a distance of forty miles or more.[37] The wagons would come about one time each week, and when they went back they would carry the wounded that were able to be moved. This was the way that we were moved from here.

Sometime in June, a raiding party of Yankees came through that section and took a part of our nurses, leaving us only a few.[38]

Our wagon train failed to come for fear of being captured. Our nurses had to look around in that raided country and pick up what they could get in the way of blackberries, cherries, and other fruits. The inhabitants divided their beans, potatoes, cabbage and other things with us, so we managed to keep alive until our train could come through in safety.

The good ladies on the other side of the river heard of our condition and a party of them got up a collection of butter and bread, and some other things, and came across the river to our hospital. They divided their nourishment among us, spoke encouraging words to us, and offered their services. We felt very grateful; but we declined their offer. I remember as one of these good ladies came in the tent where I was, gave me a piece of bread with butter, spoke kind words to me, and laid her hand on my forehead to see if I had any fever. No one knows how encouraging this was to one in our condition, and probably had not even seen a woman before in months.[39]

The wagon train began to run through regular every week, bringing rations and carrying back the wounded. The worst cases had died, but we were getting along considerably better, but not any of us wanted to stay here. Sometime in July I was considered able to be sent to the railroad train that came in on Saturday morning. On Sunday morning I was put upon an ambulance with others and bade farewell to my comrades, and left with a glad heart, after spending about one and one-half months at this place. We camped by the roadside that night. The next day we reached Orange C. H., and were taken by the way of the train to Gordonsville, and later taken to the hospital. It was time for me to be sent home but both railroads leading South from Richmond were now cut off by the enemy so I had to remain here a week or two longer. I was then furloughed by the same board that I was about one year before when I had the fever.[40] I then came home making my way by Richmond, via Danville, Greensboro and Raleigh, getting home again about the middle of July.[41]

Notes

1 Wilderness: The Battle of the Wilderness was fought May 5–7, 1864.

2 held our position: Ramseur's brigade was on duty at Rapidan Station. On May 4, the Army of the Potomac crossed the Rapidan River at several points east of the Confederate positions. On May 6, Ramseur's brigade moved southeast and aided in repulsing a Union flanking force. The 30th Regiment had seven casualties.

3 Spotsylvania Court House: The site of the Battle of Spotsylvania Court House, May 8–21, 1864, was about ten miles southeast of the Wilderness and ten miles southwest of Fredericksburg. Union control of the strategic crossroads would have opened a direct route to Richmond. After the Battle of the Wilderness, both Lee and Grant raced troops to the crossroads, with Lee's units arriving first to prepare blocking entrenchments. By May 10, over four miles of earthworks had been erected by the Confederates.

4 the enemy attacked: There were several probing attacks opposite Ramseur's position, May 8–10.

5 Horse Shoe: Known as the "Mule Shoe" in later accounts of the battle, this fortification was a salient — an outward bulge in the line designed to contain within it a patch of high ground as a favorable location for artillery. On May 10, a Union attack by five thousand men punched through the Mule Shoe at its tip, well to the right of the 30th's position, but was thrown back. Inferring a weakness at this point, Grant decided on a much bigger assault two days later.

6 towards the right: This rightward move placed the 30th Regiment on the west side — that is, the left side — of the Mule Shoe.

7 drove the men out: The dawn attack of about twenty thousand troops broke through the Mule Shoe but created a confused mass of men inside, with Union forces trying to deal with captured prisoners and secure possession of the perimeter.

8 both lines: In addition to the outer trenches of the Mule Shoe, the Confederates had constructed a partial inner line about two hundred feet back. Union forces could direct enfilading (i.e., from left and right) musket and artillery fire at the now-pushed-back Confederates.

9 take the works back: Lee was so frantic at the loss of the salient that he tried personally to lead the charge to take it back. But the men chanted, "Lee to the rear," and General John Gordon persuaded him to retreat with the promise that the Mule Shoe would be recovered.

10 In front of the shoe: Ramseur's brigade was pulled out of line, moved farther to the right, and formed behind General Junius Daniel's North Carolina brigade, in the field west of the McCoull house.

11 two ranks: A typical infantry formation would include two lines of men.

12 the first line: The inner line.   **mortally:** He means it was a wound that would normally be fatal.   **clothes on my back:** That is, his bed and clothing roll, normally worn diagonally across one shoulder and belted around the waist.

13 have the ball: It is still owned by the family. A minié ball was not an actual sphere, but a rocket-shaped hollow lead slug, invented in 1849 by a French army officer, Claude-Étienne Minié. When a musket was fired, the explosive gases filled the hollow slug, expanding it against the spiraled rifling grooves inside the barrel, propelling it outward as well as setting it rotating.

14 short distance away: The 30th Regiment was at the right end of the Ramseur brigade, near the kink in the Mule Shoe later known to history as the Bloody Angle, a scene of ghastly slaughter for twenty hours, as both sides continued to feed fresh men into the maelstrom. Although faint remnants of the trenches remain, the exact location at which JWB was hit cannot be determined.

15 another ball struck me: It appears that these subsequent strikes involved spent bullets that did not penetrate, or only slightly, since he does not afterward mention wounds other than the first one.

16 The trunk: The twenty-two-inch bullet-riddled "Spotsylvania stump" can still be seen in the National Museum of American History, part of the Smithsonian Institution.

17 formed a line: While the battle for the entrenchments around the Mule Shoe raged through the day and into the night, the Confederates frantically dug a new trench line across its base, in effect abandoning the salient. In the early-morning hours of the thirteenth, the order was given to withdraw from the Mule Shoe. JWB now lay between the lines.

18 French descent: Although this incident sounds hallucinatory, in fact there were two Louisiana brigades at the Mule Shoe on May 12. One brigade had almost every man captured when the Union forces broke through. The other brigade was in the same general area as Ramseur's brigade. Called the Louisiana Tigers, the Louisiana soldiers were a notoriously undisciplined lot, though brave and tough in battle. In response to a request for comment about this incident, Terry Jones, professor of history at the University of Louisiana at Monroe, wrote in an e-mail that it was fully believable, since "many of the Louisiana Tigers spoke only French. And many were notorious for looting the dead (and robbing the living)." See Terry L. Jones, *Lee's Tigers: The Louisiana Infantry in the Army of Northern Virginia* (Baton Rouge: Louisiana State University Press, 2002).

19 look that way: Toward the sound of the shot, to see who or what had spooked the scavengers.

20 little water: With the overwhelming thirst of the wounded, he would have quickly drunk the small amount poured in his canteen.

21 Morning again came: Saturday the fourteenth.

22 other places: The only dwelling in the Mule Shoe was the McCoull farmhouse, the foundation of which can still be seen. It was a clapboard saltbox with chimneys at both ends, two windows in front, and second-floor windows on the sides. If JWB's memory of the distance from the house to the "little hill" where he lay is accurate, it is possible that the spot was about where the monument to the Ramseur brigade is today.

23 some cannon: In the 1920 typescript, only the words "cannon" or "cannons" appear here and in following references to the cover JWB is trying to reach. The 1938 typescript, made after JWB's death, adds the word "redoubts" in each instance. A redoubt was usually a low and makeshift earthwork behind which artillery or riflemen could fire. We have decided to use the 1938 formulation. While it is possible that JWB sought shelter behind a ruined cannon on the field, he appears to be describing abandoned earthworks. The map of the battlefield made soon afterward by Confederate mapmaker Jedediah Hotchkiss shows short battery positions forward of the new Confederate infantry line on May 15. In an e-mail, Donald Pfanz, staff historian at the Fredericksburg and Spotsylvania National Military Park, wrote, "By May 14th, all Confederate artillery in that sector would have been behind Lee's final line, constructed across the base of the Mule Shoe."

24 one hour before day: The moon set at 1:27 a.m. in Virginia on Sunday, May 15, 1864. Sunrise was at 5:00 a.m., but it would have been light enough to see and take aim well before that. It appears that he had several hours of darkness in which to move, but given his condition, he could have moved only very slowly.

25 companion's knapsack: From this description, it appears that he is lugging the knapsack or haversack. It is difficult to imagine how, with a large bullet wound in his upper right chest, he could have moved with a stick in one hand and a knapsack in the other — or why he would have tried to carry the sack. Possibly he abandoned the stick he had used to pull himself up, and found another one to use for the signal.

26 moving down: In fact, Grant did not move his army until May 19, but continued to try to break through the new line at the base of the Mule Shoe. The last, futile, assault took place on the eighteenth. JWB would have been unaware of these attacks.

27 than I was: From his minimal description, the exact nature of his wound is unknowable. Eloise Bone Faison, JWB's granddaughter (1917–2009), when asked by the editors about the location of the scar that he had sometimes showed to her and her siblings, touched a spot about two inches below the right clavicle (collarbone). Dr. Peter Moyer, professor emeritus in emergency medicine at Boston University School of Medicine and former medical director of the Boston Police and Fire Emergency Medical Service, provided a written analysis: "I am assuming the shot entering 'the right breast' exited to the right of the spine (did not cross into the left thorax). The bullet did not hit his heart or a major vessel (aorta or inferior vena cava); he would not have survived. The most benign injury would have been an entirely extrathoracic injury in which the bullet passed through the skin beneath the right breast, hit a rib, and traveled outside the thoracic cage, but under the skin, to exit the skin to the right of the spine in the back. Bullets do take strange courses and this injury does occur. But I doubt it was the case for John Bone. His repeated referrals to weakness suggest a more serious injury. Assuming the bullet did enter his thoracic cavity (and didn't hit a major vessel), the most likely injuries would have been a pneumothorax (free air in the pleural space between the chest wall and lung) and/or a hemothorax — blood in that same space. The former occurs simply from the bullet passing through the lung. The latter occurs most frequently when the bullet passes through and under a rib. Under each rib is an artery and a vein. The artery is a pencil-sized vessel and part of the higher-pressure systemic circulation. A pneumothorax can occur alone or in combination with a hemothorax. Disruption of the high-pressure intercostal artery is the commonest cause of hemothorax. A small pneumothorax is quite survivable without intervention (air in the pleural space eventually resorbs on its own). The addition of a small hemothorax might also be survivable without intervention, but that is much less likely." In other words, it is possible that the bullet punched between the ribs front and back, puncturing the lung without rupturing, or fully rupturing, an intercostal artery. Or, in view of Eloise Faison's recollection of the scar, the bullet could have passed above the rib cage. Dr. Moyer wrote that "a bullet entering beneath the clavicle could certainly miss ribs and still penetrate the lung, causing a pneumothorax."

28 from death: Amazing as it sounds, recovery from just such a wound was not unprecedented. Betts described a similar case in the same regiment in his wartime diary: "'Oct. 14 [1862] — Tiresome ride to Shepardstown to see wounded men, Hathaway, Brown, Dement and Lieutenant Crews. A minié ball passed through his chest at Sharpsburg.' (I had no idea he could live; but in 1870 and 1871 I was his pastor at Oxford.)" (Betts, 20). Second Lieutenant Alexander Crews served in Company G.

29 large grove: A battlefield aid station, normally with a medical staff of about twenty, to which the wounded were taken for immediate treatment and held for later evacuation to a hospital.

30 the station: The train station.

31 where the wounded were: It appears that he has remained at an aid station near the front, and only now is being moved to "the large grove" mentioned earlier. The number — "about one thousand" — of wounded men there suggests that this is a larger facility.

32 started off: The shock of such battlefield evacuations could indeed be fatal. See p. 17, n. 20. General John Imboden, who led the seventeen-mile wagon train of Confederate wounded after the Battle of Gettysburg, wrote after the war: "Many of the wounded in the wagons had been without food for thirty-six hours . . . their torn and bloody clothing, matted and hardened, was rasping their tender, inflamed, and still oozing wounds. Very few of the wagons had even a layer of straw in them, and all were without springs. . . . The jolting was enough to have killed strong men if long exposed to it . . . no heed could be given to any of their appeals." Imboden, "The Confederate Retreat from Gettysburg," in *Battles and Leaders of the Civil War,* Vol. 3 (New York: Castle Books, 1956), 425, cited in Spencer C. Tucker, *Brigadier General John D. Imboden: Confederate Commander in the Shenandoah* (Lexington: University Press of Kentucky, 2002), 154.

33 saving my life: This was not the first time that Betts received credit for saving a life with practical advice: "July 1 [1862] — Capt. Allen's right arm was so broken up that it had to be amputated. His case will interest others. He had an idea that surgeons were fond of cutting off men's limbs. Dr. Briggs asked me to see him and try to influence him, for he refused to allow his arm amputated. Capt. Allen had lately married Miss Johns in Wake County, N. C. I prayed silently as I went to where he lay. Kneeling by him, I said, 'Capt. I long for you to get home and see that lovely young wife, who is praying for you, but you will never see her if you try to keep that arm.' We looked silently into each other's eyes. After a while, he said: 'Mr. Betts, I wish you would call Briggs to me.' I called Dr. Briggs! (Nine years after I met him in Wake. He took me to his home. Introducing me to his wife, he said, 'Bro. Betts, I want to confess to you in the presence of my wife that I owe my life to you.' The reader must imagine my feelings)" (Betts, 40).

34 lucky enough: Though he believes that God is managing the action, he also allows for the role of luck. It is undoubtedly true that lying between the lines, in relatively warm weather, with water and food, he was probably better off than he would have been in medical hands. In a strange way, the wound itself helped to save his life. If he had not been hit, it is likely he would have been killed with most of the first wave at or near the Bloody Angle. The 30th Regiment suffered forty-five killed at Spotsylvania. Also, since the bullet exited the body intact and did not hit an arm or a leg, after he made his way back to his side, there was no probing with unwashed hands or surgery with unsterilized instruments.

35 different direction: As explained in n. 23 above, the word "redoubts" was added to "cannons" in the 1938 typescript. However, in this case the words "a different direction" suggest that JWB is referring not to the sheltering redoubts but to the Union battery near the McCoull house (see p. 80) that was firing, but evidently not directly toward the spot where he was lying. Hence we have omitted the word "redoubts."

36 being sent off: The meaning is uncertain. Possibly he is thinking that the scavenger might have arranged for his evacuation had he not fled at the sound of firing.

37 Fredericksburg railroad: The Richmond and Fredericksburg Railroad was blocked by the U.S. Army to the north.

38 took a part of our nurses: This seems to mean that the nurses, being able-bodied, were taken prisoner but the wounded were left alone.

39 seen a woman: Although the exact location is not certain, the village of Massaponax Church was on the east side of the nearby Ni River. The wounded — or perhaps the medical officers in charge — decline the women's offer of "services," possibly because they are not equipped to give effective help. However, the kind and sensible touch (giving him food and checking for fever) of a woman has a comforting effect that JWB never forgets.

40 the same board: The medical review board at Gordonsville.

41 Richmond: His service record shows that on July 16, he was admitted to Receiving and Wayside Hospital in Richmond, also known as General Hospital No. 9, formerly Seabrook's Tobacco Warehouse, adjacent to the Virginia Central Railroad depot on Grace Street, between 17th and 18th streets. It was possibly only a one- or two-night stay while he waited for a train south to North Carolina on the Richmond and Danville Railroad, which departed from a depot on the river, a half-mile from the hospital. Besides medical care, the hospital provided temporary accommodations for traveling soldiers. The record also notes that he had a forty-five-day furlough, which would have expired around September 1, but evidently received a thirty-day extension, since he did not return to duty until October. At war's end, Receiving and Wayside Hospital became the home of the African American Richmond Theological Seminary, which later grew into Virginia Union University. Robert W. Waitt Jr., *Confederate Military Hospitals in Richmond* (Richmond: Official Publication No. 22, Richmond Civil War Centennial Committee, 1964).

7.

CEDAR CREEK, PETERSBURG
July 1864–April 1865

I remained until about the first of October and then made my way back to my command, which was located in a valley, near Staunton, Virginia.[1] On my way back, I had to stay over in Danville twenty-four hours for want of transportation. I reached Richmond about night, spent the night there, and started out the next day to the central road. When we passed the first station the engine jumped the track; it being so late when it was gotten back on that we went back to Richmond and stayed until the next morning. I spent the night at the station and the next morning we left for Staunton. We reached there that night, got off the train with several hundred more men of whom I scarcely knew, went out in an open field and spreading out my blanket I laid down and went to sleep. The next morning there was a big killing frost; this being October 10th.[2]

I now had to foot it down the turnpike road about eighty miles to my command. Just as I reached there the roll was sounded to fall in and march out to battle. That night I got a gun and went out to meet the enemy; but it was only cavalry, they made no stand so we went back to camp that night.[3] We remained here a few days and preparations were made for the battle of Cedar Creek.[4] One night we were commanded to give up our canteens and cups and such other things that would rattle and make a noise. The horns blew and bands played; all seemed to be in good spirits.[5]

Cedar Creek was between us and the enemy. They occupied the North side and we the South, the turnpike crossed the Creek between us at a stone bridge. Sometime that night we marched down the Creek over muddy hills. The way was so narrow and rough that we had to get in one rank and use our guns against the ground to keep from going down hill too fast, but we succeeded in getting to a desired place just before day-break. We were on the Eastside of the enemy. We waded and formed in line of battle and moved forward.[6] We were soon into their camps and had them completely routed. The troops at the bridge now crossed with our artillery, and came to our assistance. There was a big lot of plunder left on the field. We kept the enemy moving back until that evening.[7]

This was General Early's command but he was not present in the morning so General Gordon was commanding.[8] General Early came up in the evening and took command and said, "Halt", and wait until night and we will fall back; but before night the enemy was reinforced and attacked us. We were forced to fall back and many of the men got very much confused in some places and fell back in bad order.[9] General Ramseur was now our Major General. I remember seeing him that morning on his horse, just behind the line of battle when it was in the thickest of the battle. He was killed. Our brigade was one of the last to fall back. We were flanked on each side, until we came very near all being captured. When we had to give way we saw our condition and had to make the best of it. Every man was looking out for himself.[10]

I ran until I was very warm and had to stop and walk. The balls and shells were striking all around me. A ball struck between my feet, I looked back and saw the enemy's line of sharpshooters about one hundred yards back of me and their line of battle back of that. I took a trot up a hill and passed an old house where a great pile of men were behind for protection, but they were captured.[11] I thought they would get me in spite of all my efforts, but kept try-

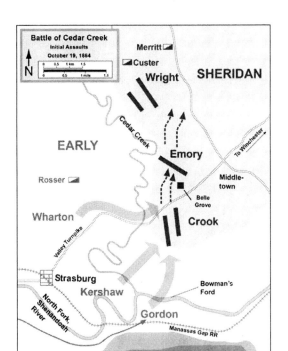

The Confederate attack at the Battle of Cedar
Creek, October 19, 1864.
(Map by Hal Jespersen, www.cwmaps.com)

ing. General Early went riding off as he saw there was no use trying
to form line of battle, and I took after him.

I soon came to the turnpike road near a bridge across a little
stream.[12] The bridge was crowded with men and wagons, but I
managed to get across, and thought I was safe; but about that time
the enemy had gotten some artillery in shape, and they opened
fire at the bridge with grape-shot and canister shells. It looked as
though they were going to kill everything in the road. I turned
from the road and went up the stream where I found some protection. I kept moving on, but I could hear men halloo out, "I am
wounded." It was about dark, and I kept on my way up the Creek

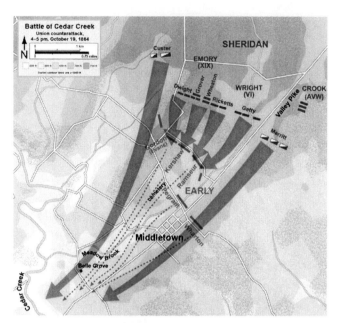

The Union counterattack at Cedar Creek.
(Map by Hal Jespersen, www.cwmaps.com)

towards the stone bridge, not knowing whether I would get to
it first before the Yankees did. I heard their cavalry run into our
wagon train ahead of me, and I thought I would go down and
wade the Creek; but knowing the steepness of the banks and the
rough hills on the other side, I kept making for the bridge.[13]

When I got near it was dark, and I could see some firelights
there. I ventured near enough to see that there was somebody
at the fire, but really could not tell who they were; but began to
believe they were Yankees. One of my comrades came up to me
and asked me who they were (the people at the bridge). About this
time we saw two men coming over to us. As they approached, I was
almost certain that they were our enemies. They spoke and asked
which side we belonged to.[14] I gave them some kind of answer, but
did not tell them for I saw they were Yankees, and did not know

but what I would be a prisoner in a short while; but I now saw that they had no guns, and I decided they would not take us.

I asked them who the people were at the fire, they told me they were prisoners that had been captured that morning, and as our army was falling back, the guards left them and they were making their way back to their side. I learned that the enemy had not reached the bridge, so they went their way and I went on and crossed the bridge. I thought I was now safe, for I soon found several of my comrades on the turnpike. Our brigade was among the last ones to leave the field. Many were wounded, killed and captured, several going through the Creek to the mountains. I found that the greater part of the army was ahead of me; but no regular commands, for the commands were scattered all along the road.

I traveled all night without finding a man I knew. The greater number of my Company being killed, wounded, captured or scattered behind. We marched all night and all day long the next day, getting to our old camps that we had left a week or two before near New Market.[15] We had not had any sleep in two days and two nights. This about ended the campaign in the valley for the war. In a few days for some reason we were ordered back down the valley and passed through the battlefield.[16] At this point there was an accident that occurred during the battle that I will mention.

The night that we marched down the creek, and the next morning as we started into battle there was a young man about my age, and one of the boys from Nash County that left in September 1861, when the Company first left and was a good soldier, moral young man and my near companion. He was mortally wounded one morning, and was taken off the field and laid beside the road with many others to be taken back, when time and chance would admit. The army was falling back and it was seen that he could not be moved, and that he would die. A comrade secured a bundle of hay and put it under his head, covered him up with blankets, and told him he must leave or be captured; his reply was, "tell my parents and friends at home to meet me in Heaven." The comrade then left him and he had to make the best of it he could. As we reached the place again we saw a new pile of earth at the spot where our comrade was left, showing a grave. A little further off lay a bundle of hay, showing that our friend was dead and buried under a Willow Tree that weeped over the place; there to remain until the great day of judgment.

We soon returned back to our old camp, this being the last trip that we took down the valley. We remained here doing picket duty, and guarding different points until sometime in December. We had but very few tents, and they were mostly such as we carried with us, and most of the men's clothes were getting very thin from exposure. We had but little protection from the cold mountain winds that were blowing down upon us. One evening they furnished us with a few days rations; it being composed of one pound of flour, and one half pound of green beef to each man for a day, and had orders to be ready to leave early the next morning.[17]

We were camped in an open field and the next morning there was about a ten inch snow on the ground, but that made no difference. We broke camp, took the turnpike road for the railroad station at Staunton, a distance of forty or forty-five miles. As we traveled the snow became a wet marsh, and began to get our feet very wet. We marched all day, and that evening we struck camp in a piece of woods. We cut down trees and made log heaps, making a fire and soaking the snow away, we spread our blankets around the heaps and laid down and went to sleep.

The next morning we started out marching again. We reached Staunton about dark, and we were wet, worried and hungry. The cars were not ready for us, so we had to stand on the streets in this condition without fire. We became very cold, but were finally put in a box car and it being closed we got warm by the heat that was produced by us. We traveled all night and a part of next day, reaching Petersburg late in the evening.[18] We were marched one mile from town and camped. The main body of General Lee's army was camping around in the trenches around here.

A military transport train on the Orange and
Alexandria Railroad.
(Library of Congress)

We were now ordered to build our winter quarters, our tools
being a few common axes and shovels. We were to build our quarters 10 by 14 out of poles, rive boards and cover, make a chimney at
one end and a door at the other, and chink the cracks with sticks
and mud.[19] Ten to twelve men were to occupy a house. We had
very comfortable quarters, and were now clothed from head to
foot, more rations were furnished us, and we felt that we were getting along very well.[20] We had to go on picket duty very often; but
I was excused from this duty, having been made "Commissary."[21]

At this place my oldest brother was assigned to my Company.
He had been in service with the juniors for some time; but was now
eighteen years old and was sent to the regular army.[22] I was very glad
to see him but hated very much that he had come to the regular
army for his health was not very good at this time, and I would have
rather for him to remain with the juniors. We were camped back as a
reserve and were subject to go anywhere at any time.

Confederate fortifications at Petersburg.
(Library of Congress)

On one occasion the enemy made an attack on the railroad
south of Petersburg, and we were ordered to go to the support of
the men that had them in check.[23] It was raining, hailing and freez-
ing, and we made all the haste we could. We had to go a distance of
about ten miles, and had to put a pontoon bridge across the river to
cross on, reaching the battle late in the evening. As we advanced the
enemy fell back and that ended the fight. We laid on the cold icy
ground that night with a little fire, and I had to draw rations for the
men during the night. Next day things had quieted down and we
returned to our quarters, and were very glad to reach there.

We remained here until the last of February, when we were
ordered below Petersburg on the Appomattox River to guard that
point; the men that had been on duty here had been sent else-

where.[24] We occupied their quarters, but they were not as good as the ones that we left. We could hear the firing of guns at all times, day or night; there being a place in the trenches below Petersburg where the lines were near each other, and there being a piece of artillery between the lines, and being orders from both sides to keep up a regular fire all the time to keep either side from getting the cannon. We had to fall in roll call night and morning, with our guns and equipments ready to march if it was necessary. We had to do very heavy picket duty.

Our company had been recruiting ever since we reached Petersburg. Some returning from home, some from hospitals, and some of the prisoners had been exchanged and come back to us. We numbered somewhere in thirty; but had no commissioned officer. As I have said before, our Captain was killed at Spotsylvania, our First Lieutenant captured, our Second Lieutenant wounded and disabled, and we did not have enough men left to be entitled to another, so we had to be commanded by an officer of another Company. We now had but few non-commissioned officers. While we were camped at Petersburg, Col. Parker came to us and resigned as Colonel on account of a wound that he received in the summer campaign.[25] The Lieutenant-Colonel was killed, and the Major was on detail, so the regiment had to be commanded by the Senior Captain.[26]

At this place sometime in March, one morning between midnight and day we were ordered to get ready and leave at once for Petersburg. We knew very well that it meant to fight; fortunately for us the officer that was sent for us lost his way, and did not find our general headquarters as early as he was expected to. Therefore we did not get the orders so early; but we were soon on the tramp. We got in about one mile of Petersburg about day break, when the fight was to commence and our presence was wanted.[27] We had the batteries open on the enemy and they had theirs open on us. Both sides had mortar cannon, the breastworks were about one hundred yards apart, each side elevating their mortars, so as to drop shells on the other's breastworks. About forty cannons were firing as fast as they could load and fire them, the shells were going up and then coming down, it being about day break, but was dark.

It was a beautiful sight, at that time, to see those shells leave the guns like a streak of fire, and go a great distance in the air. Sometimes they would explode before they would fall. We were going right under them just as fast as we well could, so we could not enjoy the scene as well as we could have if we had been standing off viewing the scene.[28] When the cannon fire opened, our lines were doubled at the works and went forward. This is what we were wanted for, but we were behind time. They reached the enemy's works and were spiked with ten foot spikes, and ours was also spiked. These spikes were to tear up both sides before the breastworks could be reached.

The men went over ours but had to turn the enemy's away before they could pass them. They were in about fifteen feet of their works, and they were doing all they could to kill our men, while they were getting the spikes away; but when they did get them away and passed, they made the Yankees get further; but they soon reinforced and drove our men back. We reached our breastworks about the time our men did. We were under heavy shelling for some time and would have been in the charge, if we had gotten there a little sooner. We missed the charge on account of the officer getting lost.[29]

As I have said the breastworks were about one hundred yards apart, and about three feet high and four feet wide, with the earth taken away in rear to the depths of about two feet up to one or two feet of the works, leaving a place so the men could sit on their feet in the trench and the works would be to our backs. Sometime it was necessary for the men to sit at them all night. Just a few feet from the works were cabin places made with logs doubled, dirt between carried on top with logs, dirt and bags of sand. These cabins had only one small hole to go into them, and they were so arranged that when the enemy got to dropping their mortar shells over in them that the men could run in their holes (that is what they called them). There was one cabin for each Company.

The picket lines were between these works. There were ditches cut and banks of dirt piled up with rifle holes at right intervals, with ditches cut from the breastworks, crooked and turned in different directions, so that the pickets could be relieved without being seen. The picket lines were very near together in some places and kept firing at each other when they could get a glimpse of each other. There were passages cut from the trenches to the rear. They were run in many directions with poles filled with dirt at many places. This was done for protection to men going to and fro, and the rations were cooked in the rear and carried to the men in the trenches; this is about as near as I can describe the trenches around Petersburg. Men stayed in them for eight or nine months, rain or shine, hot or cold. Many were taken sick in the trenches and died, while many were killed. It was a disagreeable place; but the men that stayed were regular and understood the situation had rather be there than to be in our place as we were subject to be moved to any place at any time.

After remaining here until both sides quieted down, we were taken back. We only left the men that were on picket duty and if the enemy had known, they could have driven our pickets back and captured our quartermaster commissary and advanced wagon trains, but we reached them before they learned the situation.

Our brigade was now commanded by General W. R. Cox, and our division commanded by General Bryan Grimes.[30] We remained at our quarters until the last of March, but were in great dread all the time, not knowing at what hour we would be called to go. We realized that a place in the trenches would be good if not better than our present situation. Our cause looked very hopeless, but we continued to hope, feeling that we would succeed. We had a little hope that France would recognize us and could hear flattering encouragement, but to no avail. Great many of our men deserted us and went over to the Yankees, and some would quit and go home, but not many of such were good soldiers.[31] At this time things looked very sad and gloomy, but we knew nothing else to do but to stay and see the result, though it might end in death for most of us.

About the last of March, we were ordered in front of Petersburg, and occupied some old quarters in rear of the works near the crater, and did heavy picket duty, and were subject to be ordered anywhere along the line at any time.[32] Near the place where we now occupied was a tunnel mined under the ground. It was one-half mile long and led to a large dwelling that stood between the lines and a charge of powder placed under the house, with a means to fire it at any time should the enemy occupy the house.

On Friday night, March 31st, Grant commenced cannonading up and down the lines, and on the next day, April 1st, made some attacks.[33] We laid in the breastworks nearly all of the time, expecting to be attacked, but were not.

On Sunday morning, April 2nd, there was a heavy attack made on our right, and a part of our division was heavily engaged for a short while. The point that we held was almost in front of the town, and being a very important place, it was expected to be attacked at any time.[34] In the evening a number of sharpshooters (I being one of them) were sent out in front, and engaged the enemy's line and skirmished about until dark. We were moved to another place and placed upon picket duty in a small undergrowth, which we found uncomfortable, as the grass and sticks caused us to move slowly. We were posted in a whisper and told not to speak louder than that, and also not to fire unless we saw somebody.

It was not very long before we heard someone talking in front of us, and we could tell that they were not far off. After awhile our officer had orders to relieve us. He came to us and told each in a whisper to fall in behind him, which we did in a hurry. Those that he did not reach were captured and made prisoners. We marched back to the rear where our men were in the works, but much to our surprise we did not find anyone. Up to this time we did not know our situation, and we had been forced to fall back. We at last realized that we could not hold the place any longer, so we fled, leaving Petersburg to be captured by our enemies.[35] This place had been the headquarters for the army of Northern Virginia for the last nine months. We had to give up everything and the things that we could carry we nearly lost in our hurried flight.

We continued to march on toward the town, but very slowly as we had had a hard days fight. There was a man that was relieved when we were who made a little stop at the breastworks to look around where he had left his comrades when he went off on the sharpshooters line that day, and as he lingered a little, he saw some men coming down the works and found that it was the enemy and made his escape, so we came very near being captured. The men that were captured at this place were later on sent to Point Lookout and elsewhere and kept for several months.

We came on through the town, the people of the place seemed to be under great excitement on account of our leaving. We now began to realize our condition. We marched through the town and crossed the Appomattox River and took up the river road and after awhile reached our command.[36]

Notes

1 made my way back: JWB does not say, and the reader can only imagine, how difficult to accept this last wartime departure must have been for his parents, given the severity of the wound that had brought him home.   **Staunton:** The regiment, now part of General Jubal Early's command, was south of Middletown in the Shenandoah Valley, about eighty miles northeast of Staunton.

2 October 10th: That he returned to his regiment only five months after a massive chest wound, at a time when Confederates were deserting in droves, is testimony to his sense of duty. However, Eric T. Dean notes that duty was not always the only impetus in such cases: "Although concerned with the welfare of family and, at times, yearning to be with loved ones at home, the attitude of the Civil War soldier was also marked by a curious transformation in which he began to look at life at home as irrelevant or boring. . . . This attitude is seen more clearly in the feelings of men on home leave during the war; they were initially over-joyed to see relatives and to be at home again, but this bliss quickly gave way to tension, and eagerness for news from the front, and a desire to return to their unit to share the fate of their comrades. One sees these sentiments expressed again and again, by Union and Confederate soldiers alike." Eric T. Dean, *Shook Over Hell: Post-Traumatic Stress, Vietnam, and the Civil War* (Cambridge: Harvard University Press, 1997), 87–88.

3 that night: The date is uncertain. If it took four days to walk the eighty miles from Staunton, it was October 14.

4 battle: The Battle of Cedar Creek, or Battle of Belle Grove, took place October 19, 1864, near the towns of Strasburg and Middletown. It was the culminating engagement of the Shenandoah Valley Campaign of 1864.

5 horns blew and bands played: Regiments did have bands and horns. However, in this instance, where the men have been ordered to keep silent, it is unlikely that music would be played. JWB may mean this as a figure of speech, to show that the soldiers were eager for action

6 We waded: JWB is conflating two waterways. Cedar Creek is a winding, generally north-south tributary of the North Fork of the east-west Shenandoah River. The town of Middletown is north of the Shenandoah. The Union positions were east of the creek and north of the river. Major General John Brown Gordon's three divisions, including Ramseur's division, crossed the Shenandoah, not Cedar Creek, on the night of October 18 at a shallow spot called Bowman's Ford. Other Confederate units crossed Cedar Creek. The surprise attack commenced in the early-morning hours of the nineteenth. Surprise was aided by heavy fog soon joined by gun smoke.

7 that evening: The Confederates surprised Union forces under the command of General Horatio G. Wright and drove them more than a mile northwest of Middletown. Ramseur's division, including the N.C. 30th, pushed farther than any other unit in this battle, to a point just northeast of what is now Cougill Road, State Route 634.

8 Early: Lieutenant General Jubal Early (1816–1894) commanded the Confederates' last invasion of the North in the Valley Campaigns of 1864.

9 bad order: That is, they were routed. Early did not expect a counterattack and ordered troops to halt, at which time they began plundering Union camps. That gave the Union army time to regroup and counterattack, rallied by General Philip Sheridan (1831–1888), who rode ten miles from Winchester at the sound of firing. The Union victory stopped the Confederate advance toward Washington. "Sheridan's Ride," a romantic poem written right after the battle by painter and poet Thomas Buchanan Read, was used to promote the war effort and, by some accounts, helped reelect Lincoln a few weeks later.

10 looking out for himself: Ramseur's brigade was nearly surrounded and rushed southward to the Valley Turnpike to escape across Cedar Creek toward Strasburg.

11 old house: The Jedediah Hotchkiss post-battle map (No. 29, "Battle of Belle Grove or Cedar Creek") shows a few small structures in this area, but it is possible that JWB is describing the Belle Grove stone plantation house, which still stands on a hilltop.

12 bridge across a little stream: JWB's account of his flight is understandably confused and reflects the disorder of the rout. It would seem unlikely that he reached the Valley Turnpike (now Virginia Route 11) at this point, since he says his unit has been flanked on both sides. If so, there would have been Union troops between him and the turnpike. Also, the turnpike did not cross a stream hereabouts, but passed through the center of Middletown on Main Street. He does not mention the town. These facts suggest that he was eventually fleeing on, or alongside, Meadow Mills Road (now State Road 624) in a southwesterly direction, parallel to the town and turnpike, which were on his left. Meadow Brook, a small tributary to Cedar Creek, meanders through this area, and Meadow Mills Road crosses it just west of Belle Grove. According to the Hotchkiss map, the Cox brigade, which included the N.C. 30th, had passed through this area during the advance earlier in the day. Thus it seems probable that this was the bridge across the "small stream." Leaving the road at this point and making his way toward the "stone bridge" crossing the turnpike, he would have turned left and run southward, with Cedar Creek on his right, through what is still a thick wood on a high ridge (which indeed has steep banks down to the creek).

13 our wagon train: Union cavalry under Brigadier General George A. Custer (1839–1876) pursued the retreating Confederates along a road north of the battlefield (the area is now sullied by huge limestone quarries), which joined the turnpike west of the creek. It is not clear what JWB is hearing, though it might have been Custer's troopers; they captured a large part of the Confederate train near Strasburg, farther west.   **the bridge:** Apparently the substantial Valley Turnpike bridge over Cedar Creek, illustrated on Hotchkiss map No. 29. The map shows the "D. Stickley" farm west of the bridge. The Stickley house survives, near the modern bridge.

14 asked which side: By this late date in the conflict, many Confederate soldiers lacked uniforms that would be recognizable to Union soldiers. Some had no uniforms at all. In addition, during the rout at Cedar Creek, JWB carried no musket that would identify him.

15 New Market: New Market is thirty-three miles south of Strasburg.

16 passed through the battlefield: On November 11, Confederate troops moved northward again, passing through Middletown, near the point of the farthest advance, October 19. Union forces did not challenge them, however, and they soon returned to New Market.

17 green beef: Probably salted beef, as this was the only way to preserve meat.

18 in the evening: The forlorn trainload of cold, hungry, and mostly shoeless men in Cox's brigade left Staunton on December 15 and arrived in Petersburg the night of the sixteenth. The rail distance, via Gordonsville and Richmond, was about 230 miles.

19 rive boards: rough-sawn planks.

20 along very well: The winter quarters were at Dunlop's Station, north of the Appomattox River in what is now the Colonial Heights neighborhood.

21 Commissary: In charge of distributing rations and other supplies.

22 regular army: Henry Bone (1845–1931) was the oldest of John's three younger brothers. If he had been assigned to the regular army as soon as he turned eighteen, it would have happened the year before. The Junior Reserves included seventeen-year-olds.

23 in check: This is the Battle of Hatcher's Run, southwest of Petersburg, on February 5–7, 1865, a Union attempt to cut Confederate supply lines and capture supplies. The attack was repulsed, but Confederate losses, including the death of General John Pegram, were costly, and the Union siege lines were strengthened.

24 sent elsewhere: If "below Petersburg" means downstream on the Appomattox River, it would be on the east side.

25 and resigned: Taylor writes (p. 361) that there is no other record of this visit to the troops. Parker had been shot in the abdomen at Spotsylvania. Although he survived the war (he died in 1905 at age seventy-seven), he never returned to field duty.

26 Senior Captain: The lieutenant colonel is William Sillers, killed the previous November at the Second Battle of Rappahannock Station. The identity of the absent major is uncertain. Captain David C. Allen commanded the 30th Regiment until the surrender.

27 the fight: This is the March 25 Battle of Fort Stedman, east of Petersburg, an attempt to seize the Union-held fort and split Grant's siege. As at Cedar Creek, the initial attack succeeded, but the counterattack drove the Confederates back with heavy losses.

28 viewing the scene: JWB appears to be describing what he saw, and yet the regiment was late to the scene of action. Presumably, however, shells exploding in air would have been visible from a distance.

29 we missed the charge: JWB describes fighting in which he did not participate. Taylor writes (p. 364) that the brigade, including the 30th Regiment, "arrived at the trenches only in time to cover the Confederate withdrawal from Fort Stedman."

30 Cox and Grimes: William R. Cox (1832–1919) was appointed brigadier general after Spotsylvania. Bryan Grimes (1828–1880) became major general after the death of Ramseur at Cedar Creek.

31 good soldiers: More than 750 North Carolina soldiers deserted and surrendered between October 1864 and February 1865. Mark A. Weitz, *More Damning than Slaughter: Desertion in the Confederate Army* (Lincoln: University of Nebraska Press, 2005), 252. In his usual generous manner toward comrades, JWB does not condemn the deserters, and even seems to allow that some were good soldiers.

32 the crater: On July 30, 1864, Union forces exploded a huge mine under Confederate lines on the east side of Petersburg. However, the attackers who rushed in to exploit the gap were disorganized, and the Confederate counterattack drove them back with 3,800 casualties, including 500 killed. General Ambrose Burnside was relieved of his command in the aftermath of the disaster.

33 Grant: Lieutenant General Ulysses S. Grant (1822–1885).

34 point that we held: Cox's brigade now occupied a line of entrenchments south of the city, near a position known as Battery 45.

35 our enemies: On April 2, the army was ordered to abandon the lines and retreat north through the city.

36 crossed the Appomattox: Grimes's division crossed at Campbell's Bridge, now part of Route 36, and trekked west along River Road. The river bridges were burned after the crossing, to delay Union pursuers. There were many stragglers and it appears that JWB is among a group of soldiers separated from the regiment until after the crossing.

8.

APPOMATTOX

April 1865

The whole army was now on the march.[1] We had to move very slowly, so as to let the artillery and wagon train move on before us. We marched all night and the next day, only stopping at short intervals. I think we stopped and formed line of battle one time during the day and waited for the wagon train to move on ahead. I remember going to sleep at times walking along and would step into a hole or hit my foot against something and wake up. We were so sleepy that we could stand still and go fast asleep. Tuesday morning came and we were still moving.[2] When the men had anything to eat, they had to eat it raw or get a pan or skillet and stop off to one side and cook a bit and then move on and overtake their command.

General Lee ordered a lot of rations to be shipped from Danville, Virginia to a station on the Danville and Richmond railroad for us. When we got there we found that by some means the cars had carried it on to Richmond and it was taken by the enemy.[3] We thought that it was a Yankee trick. It would happen this way sometimes at night, while we would be marching we would come to where the roads forked and somebody posted there as a guide would tell us to take the wrong road. A time or so the army was misled by men in disguise and would go in a direction for the enemy to capture us, but would find out better and retrace our steps, which would delay us some. At one time, as the wagon train was going down into a little creek, there sat two men on horses wearing gray uniforms that ranked them as quartermaster and doctor, who ordered us to stop our wagons and let the horses drink, then drive on and let the next horses do likewise, but it was stopping the whole army and giving the enemy a chance to gain on us. It was found out later that these officers were Yankees in Confederate uniforms. Something like this would turn up very often along the way.[4]

Tuesday night came on, and we stopped part of the night, but was up and going before day.[5] It was here that we drew some rations, the first that we had drawn since we had left Petersburg.[6] We had a fight one time during the day. The enemy's cavalry would run into our wagon train and we would have to drive them away, while we were doing this, the enemy's infantry would come up with some artillery, and we would fight them awhile, thus giving the wagon train a chance to get ahead. We would leave the enemy after giving them a few rounds, and march on for awhile. We had a fight with the enemy about every day, and some days three or four times.[7]

As I have said before, my brother was in feeble health. He had been detailed to look after the horse that the Captain rode that commanded the regiment. He did not have to carry a gun or box, but had to walk nearly all the time, only when we would get into a fight, and he then would have to take the horse to the rear and bring him back again, when the fight was over. On Thursday we made rapid progress, as the roads were smooth and dry. During the day, as we stopped a few minutes to rest for the train to move on, my brother came up to me and told me that he had gone about as far as he could, and would be obliged to give up. (There was no chance for him to ride.) This was very sad and trying to me as I knew if he could not go that he would soon be captured, and what would be the result I knew not, but for me to stay with him meant being captured, and as I did not want that to happen, if I could help it, and too I knew I could not do my brother much good, if I stopped with him, so when we were ordered to march I continued on leaving him by the roadside. Will say right here that my brother was captured and paroled and reached home a few days after I did.[8]

We marched all day, and late in the evening the enemy caught up with us. We reached a creek or river, the banks were steep in most places, but the stream was shallow, I think there was a bridge or ford to the county road, but the wagon and artillery kept that occupied.[9] There was a railroad crossing near the same place.[10] The railroad bridge was opened, and said to be a wire bridge and nearly one hundred feet high, and one-fourth of a mile long. The men were crossing on it. When I reached the bridge, it was packed as full as it could be from one end to the other, so full that the men could not move fast. About the time I reached it, the men that had reached the middle became excited thinking that the bridge was giving way and they were almost in a panic, but could not do anything but gradually move on or jump off the bridge, not many tried the latter, and the bridge did not fall. I with many others did not go on it, but went below and waded, and got across sooner than we would if we had crossed the bridge. We traveled a portion of the night before we stopped. While here we drew some rations. Our bread material was one ear of corn to the man. I remember marching, and shelling and eating mine raw, and it was good too.

The next day, Friday, we reached Farmville, Virginia, formed line of battle, fought awhile, moved on, and formed line again, made breastworks with fence rails and dirt, and fought again.[11] I was by the side of a piece of artillery while it was firing, which was very annoying. I could hardly hear after the firing was over. We stopped the enemy and moved on again. I do not recollect how many engagements that we had during the day, but several of the men were being captured. It was now very plain that the cause was hopeless.

Saturday morning, April 8th, found us tramping on, we marched all day without any engagements, having gotten ahead of

The High Bridge over the Appomattox River in 1865, near
Farmville, photographed by Timothy H. O'Sullivan.
(Library of Congress)

the enemy the night before. (When the sun was about one hour
high.) In the evening we stopped, stacked arms and drew rations.
We now had a chance to cook and eat a square meal. It was a
beautiful evening, but a little cool. After eating, we laid down to
sleep, hoping to have one more night's rest. Sometime between
midnight and day, we were aroused, fell in line, took up our arms,
and marched off. About light we were halted (we were now at
Appomattox Court House) and were soon formed into line of
battle, and charged the enemy and drove them back.[12] I think we
made three charges on the enemy before getting them away from
our wagon train; it being mostly cavalry we were fighting.[13]

Things now looked still darker, but we had no idea that we
were so near the end. General Cox marched his brigade westward
into a piece of woods, formed line of battle and went forward into
an open field. At the back side of the field, about one-fourth of a

mile away, we saw a heavy line of the enemy in line of battle. We were ordered to fire on them by front rank. The enemy did not fire on us. We were expecting a heavy fight right here, but as soon as we discharged our guns, we were ordered to march back to the rear. As we were marching back to the rear a bullet came from somewhere and struck one of the regiment and killed him after he had passed through the struggle and was making the last retreat. Everywhere it is believed that our brigade fired the last gun that was fired by the Confederates at Appomattox.[14] We marched back a piece, not knowing or thinking that General Lee had surrendered. We stacked arms and commenced piling up some fence rails for protection, expecting to be attacked soon. While we were at this somebody passed by us and said "That Lee had surrendered," but we did not think it was so.

We were soon ordered to fall in, and we were marched over a little hill and down into a large field. We now began to believe the report, for we could see our wagon train standing together and the enemy before them. It was here that we learned for certain that the army of Northern Virginia had surrendered. We stacked arms and laid down and to rest. This was about ten o'clock Sunday, April 9th, 1865.[15] We had been tramping and fighting for one week. We supposed that it would have been better to have surrendered at Petersburg, but many would have said that we did not do all that we could.

General Lee's plans were to reach the Virginia railroad and get his army to unite with General Johnston's, which was then near Greensboro, N.C., and then make a stand.[16] But after leaving Petersburg and missing the supplies and finding how close that we were pursued, he realized that our cause was hopeless and began to try to make some terms of surrender. When agreement was made we were to be paroled and returned to our homes, carrying with us what was ours individually and remain there undisturbed until we were duly exchanged.[17]

General Robert E. Lee's return to Confederate
lines after signing the surrender.
(British Library)

Sometime in the evening we marched off a short distance, each
division and brigade camping together as they generally did. It was
here that we used the last rations we had on hand, and the last we
ever got from the Confederacy. The enemy camped near us, and we
were soon visiting each other's camps. I suppose that most of us on
both sides took the quietest night rest that we had in many, for we
were not dreading and watching for each other; for the lion and the
lamb had now laid down together.[18]

I could not find but three more present, beside myself, of the
first old original Company that left Nash County in September,
1861. One of them had not been in battle or fired a gun in the
services. (He having a deficiency was kept on detail.) Another was
only fifteen, when he went off, and had been kept on detail most of
the time, and had not been in but a few fights. The other one had
done good service a part of the time, had been twice wounded and
remained in prison about fourteen months. I was the only one of
the old Company that surrendered that had been with the Company most of the time and that had not been on detail and kept

from the battles. There were others of the old Company living, some in prison, on detail, and at home. Our Company, when they surrendered numbered eighteen, having lost nearly half of what it numbered when we left Petersburg.[19]

It was considered best to parole the cavalry first, so that they could get their horses away, where they could be fed. We remained here in camp Monday and Tuesday waiting for our paroles. On Tuesday evening General Lee had us marched out and had all of his men gathered as near together as they well could be; then he and others rode in the midst of us, and then setting on his horse, pulled off his hat, and made a speech, telling us of his regrets that we had not succeeded in gaining the cause that we had tried so hard for, but did not put the blame on us, complimented us for the four years of hard services that we had done, and also told us to go home in peace, be good citizens, and try to rebuild our lost fortunes. He sadly bade us all and the army of Northern Virginia adieu, and departed from us for the last time.[20]

We went back to our camps and remained that night, it being the last night that the army camped together. We spent the night in various ways, some sang and prayed, some sat around the camp fires and told their war jokes, some sung the war songs that had been so familiar with us, others talked of home sweet home that they soon expected to see, and we all slept a little. As for me, I was called out on duty, being the last and only man in my command that did duty at Appomattox.[21]

The next morning we received our paroles, and were commanded to fall in with all of our equipments for the last time, and marched out in an open field where there was a line of Yankees, I don't know how long.[22] They had no arms and the commission officer was in charge of them.[23] We fronted them, and were commanded by our officer to stack arms, and take off our cartridge boxes, belts, and hang them on their arms. We obeyed the command, and this was the last command that we received.

The last stacking of arms at Appomattox.
(National Park Service)

We said nothing to those that had been our enemies, neither did they say anything to us. We were marched off some distance, told to break rank, and go to our homes in peace. We cannot express our feelings nor can others realize them at this point, not that we rejoiced, for it was a solemn time with us. We had known for four years that military discipline was connected with go and come at its command and take what it gave us to eat and wear. During that time we had made many friends and acquaintances.

Notes

1 The whole army: The Army of Northern Virginia moved west along several routes, pursued and harassed by Union forces.

2 Tuesday: April 4.

3 taken by the enemy: Grimes's division, including Cox's brigade, reached Amelia Court House, a stop on the Danville and Richmond Railroad, on Wednesday, April 5. Lee had planned for the wings of his retreating army to meet there, resupply with stores sent east by rail from Lynchburg, and move on. But the supplies never arrived.

4 along the way: It is not clear that he witnessed this incident. It is a fact, in any case, that the army was slowed by the movement of the baggage and supply wagons, as horses had to stop and drink at streams where soldiers needed to pass.

5 before day: Wednesday, April 5.

6 we drew some rations: Since supplies had not arrived at Amelia Court House, these rations must have been from the remaining store carried by the army.

7 three or four times: Grant's army was gradually overtaking and surrounding Lee's force.

8 brother was captured: Henry was a prisoner of war at Farmville for about a month.

9 creek or river: The Appomattox River.

10 railroad crossing: There were two bridges at this site, northeast of Farmville. The "bridge or ford" was a low wooden bridge for wagons and pedestrians. The High Bridge was a wood-frame rail trestle set on a row of stone piers. A replacement rail bridge built later at the site, alongside the old piers, today is used as a bicycle crossing in High Bridge Trail State Park.

11 Friday: April 7.   **Farmville:** A town on the Southside Railroad seventy miles from Petersburg, thirty miles from Appomattox.

12 About light: Sunday morning, April 9.

13 our wagon train: The Union forces were blocking the road west toward Lynchburg. The attack drove them from the road, but more numerous Union formations beyond soon became apparent.

14 Everywhere it is believed: Taylor writes that the last man killed was Sergeant Ivey Ritchie of Company H, not killed by a bullet but by a bursting artillery shell. There are conflicting accounts of which Confederate unit fired the last individual shot at Appomattox, but Taylor (pp. 370–6) concludes that Cox's brigade fired the last volley.

15 April 9th: The actual surrender, at the Wilmer McLean homestead, occurred in the afternoon. A truce had been declared so that Lee and Grant could meet to discuss terms.

16 Johnston: General Joseph E. Johnston (1807–1891), whom Lee had succeeded as commander of the Army of Northern Virginia three years before, surrendered to General William T. Sherman in North Carolina on April 26.

17 duly exchanged: It was not certain that the war was over (the last Confederate force surrendered in June) and that there would be no more fighting. Terms written by Grant at the surrender included the provision that "the officers to give their individual paroles not to take up arms against the Government of the United States until properly exchanged; and each company or regimental com-

mander sign a like parole for the men of their commands." The parole pass given
to the enlisted men did not mention exchanges.

18 the lion and the lamb: Isaiah 11: 6–7. "The wolf also shall dwell with the
lamb, and the leopard shall lie down with the kid; and the calf and the young
lion and the fatling together; and a little child shall lead them."

19 left Petersburg: Taylor writes that 153 men of the 30th Regiment, including
seven officers, surrendered (378).

20 departed from us: Lee did not actually leave for Richmond until late
in the day of the surrender ceremony, April 12. Confederate general Edward
Porter Alexander recalled years later that the men swarmed around Lee after he
returned from the meeting with Grant at the McLean home on the morning
of April 9. "Now, he told the men in a few words that he had done his best for
them & advised them to go home & become as good citizens as they had been
soldiers. As he spoke a wave of emotion seemed to strike the crowd & a great
many men were weeping, & many pressed to shake his hand & to try & express
in some way the feelings which shook in every heart." *Fighting for the Confederacy: The Personal Recollections of General Edward Porter Alexander,* Gary W. Gallagher, ed. (Chapel Hill: University of North Carolina Press, 1989), 539–40. The
next day, Lee issued a formal valedictory to the army in General Order No. 9,
sometimes referred to as Lee's Farewell. JWB here describes a verbal message to
the troops on Tuesday, the eleventh, which is surprising in that Lee had already
given almost this identical message in writing. Possibly JWB is conflating the
encounter on Sunday with Order No. 9. However, some accounts do describe
Lee speaking to his veterans more than once, and he could have reiterated his
earlier message.

21 in my command: Presumably sentry duty. It is not clear if he means the last
in the company or the regiment. The latter seems more likely, given how few
were left.

22 paroles: The parole was a strip of paper, about three by six inches, printed
at Appomattox and given to the soldiers. JWB's parole, which has not survived,
would have read, *"THE BEARER,* John W. Bone, *of* Co. I, 30th *Regt. of* North
Carolina, *a Paroled Prisoner of the Army of Northern Virginia, has permission to go
to his home, and there remain undisturbed."* It would have been signed by Captain
D. C. Allen, in command of the 30th.

23 had no arms: By all accounts the men of the 1st Division of the Union
Fifth Corps, lined up to accept the surrender on the village square, did carry
arms. They famously were ordered by General Joshua Chamberlain to "present arms" — hold their muskets vertically in front of their chests in a gesture
of respect — and General John Gordon, leading the Confederates, reportedly
dipped his sword in acknowledgment. It is possible that some part of the Union
company present, visible to JWB, did not carry arms.

9.

WALKING HOME

We were turned out into the world most of us without any money, with one weather-beaten suit of clothes, and nothing to eat, entirely on the mercy of somebody else. The Government had not paid us any wages in over twelve months, and most of us were from one hundred to one thousand miles from home.[1] With all of these disadvantages against us, we were in sad condition, but we were very glad to take the chance, hoping that we could once more reach our homes, that we had not seen in a long time, and see a friend once again.

General Cox called the attention of his brigade, and complimented us for our faithfulness, telling us of the many hard battles we had fought, and charged the enemies in large numbers at his command, and carried them before us when we were greatly outnumbered. He also told us as long as he had a home any member of his brigade would be welcome, and he then told us to go to our homes in peace. He said to ask people of means for something to eat, and if the people would not give us of their means to take enough to get along with; but to treat the people with great respect. He then bided us adieu, and mounted his horse and rode off.[2]

As I have said before there were eighteen of us that surrendered. We decided that we would all stay together, and try to make our way home.[3] It was a very solemn time when we began to scatter and start for our homes in different directions. We lived in various places, and we knew that we would probably never see each other again, and this made the farewell very sad to say to our friends. As we told each other good-bye, you could hear all around these words: Remember how we laid and bled together on the battlefield, or side by side in the hospital, or through the cold winter in some prison. Many of us have not seen or heard from each other since that morning.

Eighteen of us started for North Carolina. We did not travel by command or in ranks, as we had been so used to doing. We traveled for some distance, and began to think about something to eat, for I don't know if any of us had had anything to eat that day. To my best recollection, while we were with the Yankees they gave us two crackers and a little pickle beef to the man. They would have doubtless given us more if they could have done so without taking from themselves.[4]

We now saw a nice looking settlement near the side of the road, and we approached it. We found the owner was a Baptist preacher. We made our wants known to him, and he told us that the Yankees had plundered his place, and took most everything that he had to eat, but would divide what he had with us. In a short time he had some boiled Irish potatoes and parched corn brought out and spread down before us, and told us this was the best that he could do. He and his boys ate with us. We thanked him very kindly and bidded him good-bye.

We traveled all day, and that evening we came to an old vacant house by the roadside and camped for the night. We made our breakfast and supper from a piece of bacon and some meal. This was Wednesday night. The next morning we started on the road again, and about noon we came to another house beside the road.[5] A widow woman lived here, she was standing on the porch, and asked us to come in and get some milk and bread, which we did and we were very glad to get that. She said that her son had reached home that morning and how thankful she was. She also said that she was glad to give us something, for she would have been thankful for her son to have been treated the same way. We continued on and crossed the Richmond and Danville railroad about night.[6] This was a poor and thinly settled country, but we traveled on until dark. When we came to the County Home for the poor, we made our wants known to the superintendent, who took us in and gave us some supper and a room to sleep in.

Friday morning we were on the road very early. We began to scatter here, most of the men taking the Southern roads, and the rest took the Eastern roads. In the afternoon we passed through the little town of Marysville, and we were given a piece of bacon, some corn meal, and syrup, which we made our supper and breakfast from, camping beside the road that night.[7] Saturday we reached the Roanoke river at Taylor's Ferry, and were carried across in a big float by two Negroes.[8] They demanded one dollar per head, which we gave them; this was the last Confederate money that I spent. It rained that evening very hard, and when we came to a vacant house with a chimney to it, we stopped, made a fire and dried our clothes. Near night it stopped raining, and ten of our crowd left for home, leaving eight of us, who did not feel like traveling any further that day.

Sunday morning we started again, passing Warren Plain and through Warrenton.[9] We stopped a few miles from Warrenton at one of Major Buck Williams' plantations, our former quartermaster, and we were given supper and a room to sleep in by the foreman.[10]

Early the next morning we left, making our way homeward, feeling that we were nearing the desired goal. After an hour or two's travel, we came to a large farm. The owner was by the road-side attending his stock. He saluted us, asking us where our homes were. On being told he commenced counting us and called a boy, and told him to go to the house and tell his mistress to prepare breakfast for so many men, then remarked that you have not had any this morning, and we told him no. He took us to the house. (He was Mr. Cheek and the father of Dr. Cheek, the surgeon of the 22nd Regiment.)[11] The Doctor had just reached home the night before, and gave us a warm welcome. Mr. Cheek told us that he was the owner of one hundred Negroes, and that he did not regret to lose them in case that he should. (The Negroes were not free then, but we were very certain that they would soon be.)[12]

Breakfast was announced and we all entered the dining room. After asking the blessing, he said, "gentlemen, this is your breakfast, do as you please with it." We thanked him, and then kindly asked his family to eat with us, which they did. He told us lots of good jokes during the time that we remained with him. As we were getting ready to take our departure, he asked us to listen to another story or illustration.

He said, "There was once two good young men that were very strong friends, and who always tried to do right. One of them was taken sick and was very certain that he would die, the other one went to see him and they talked matters over, of their past lives, and that the sick one would soon die and be taken to Heaven, the other telling him that when he got there to tell the people there about him, then bade him adieu until they met in a better land. After leaving his companion, the thought came to him that his friend might not get to the better land, so he turned about and went back and said, should you not get to the better place, don't let the people know anything about me, don't let them know that there is such a fellow as I. So now when you soldiers leave here and you meet with your comrades, don't tell them anything about me, don't let them know that there is such a fellow as Cheek." We all enjoyed a good laugh, and bade him adieu, and got on the road for home feeling that soon we would reach our loved ones, who we knew were very anxious to know of our welfare.

We traveled about all day, and late in the evening reached Nash County, at the place then known as Porter's Gold Mine, near Hilliardston.[13] As I have before said there were eight of us together, the other ten leaving us soon after we crossed the Roanoke. We had come all the way together from Appomattox, but we must now be separated, for three of the eight lived in the Western part of the County, and it was necessary for them to take different roads.

I will now try to state our condition. There were two married men among us, one of them had a good home, the other had no home of his own, another was a very intelligent young man, but had neither home or parents and but few relatives. Another was a young fellow not grown and had no parents, but near relations. As for me, I found my father and mother, and two young brothers all living at the old homestead and in very good circumstances for war times.

At this writing, I am the only one of the eight that is living, and there is only about one of the eighteen that surrendered now living. Will say here, that we had more men in our Company at the surrender than almost any other Company. The cause for this was that we had nearly all of our Company taken as prisoners. As I have before stated they had been exchanged only a short time before the war ended. It was sad to leave our comrades and bid them good-bye after being together so long and go out to battle with life in our sad condition. It was now Monday evening, and we traveled on until night, reaching the home of Thomas Cooper, a former acquaintance, and an ex-sheriff of Nash County who gave us a good lodging for the night. On the next morning after eating breakfast, we departed for our homes passing through Nashville, the County seat, the place where we had left four years before. I reached my home that evening, and found all well.[14] My brother returned in a few days.

I WROTE THIS IN THE YEAR 1904, while confined in bed with rheumatism and in my free hours from pain would lie and write. Should anyone read these lines, they may ask why I could remember them after a lapse of forty years. Will say in answer that the hardships, sufferings, and thoughts of death, with many other things are formed so strong in my mind that they will never be forgotten as long as I have a clear mind. Besides, as I lie and travel the road over, many things come to my mind that had passed my recollection and many things that occurred I have not mentioned.[15]

J. W. Bone

Notes

1 from home: The distance between Appomattox Court House and Nashville, North Carolina, is about 150 miles.

2 rode off: Cox had a substantial postwar career, including the presidency of the Chatham Railroad, a state judgeship, three terms in Congress, and appointment as secretary of the U.S. Senate. At his death in 1919, he was one of the last surviving Confederate generals.

3 make our way home: "For many days afterwards all the roads in the state were full of weary men wending their way homewards." Joseph A. Waddell, *Annals of Augusta County Virginia: From 1726 to 1871* (Staunton, Va: Russell Caldwell, 1902).

4 given us more: In his memoirs, Grant wrote that Lee had asked for rations for his men, who "had been living for some days on parched corn exclusively." Grant then "authorized him to send his own commissary and quartermaster to Appomattox Station, where he could have, out of the trains we had stopped [i.e., captured Confederate trains], all the provisions wanted." Ulysses S. Grant, *Personal Memoirs of U. S. Grant, Vol. 2* (New York: Charles Webster and Co., 1886), 495. Freeman, Lee's biographer, quotes Grant as saying, "Suppose I send over 25,000 rations, do you think that will be a sufficient supply?" Lee replied, "I think it will be ample." Douglas Southall Freeman, *Lee: An Abridgement by Richard Harwell* (New York: Scribners, 1991), 493. However much was sent, and from what stores, JWB's memory suggests that it did not add up to a generous portion per man. Yet he does not complain.

5 next morning: Thursday, April 13, the day after the surrender.

6 crossed the Richmond: The Richmond and Danville Railroad was 140 miles long. JWB probably crossed near Drake's Branch, about thirty miles southeast of Appomattox.

7 Marysville: Marysville is the former name of Charlotte Court House, county seat of Charlotte County, about twenty miles south of Appomattox.

8 Roanoke river at Taylor's Ferry: A ferry was operating at this location before 1760, when the right to keep the ferry was purchased by Edmund Taylor, who then owned the location of the ferry landing. It became known as Taylor's Ferry and operated for more than 150 years. The Roanoke River was dammed in 1952 at a narrow point south of Boydton, obliterating the location of Taylor's Ferry.

9 Warrenton: Warrenton is about thirty miles southeast of Boydton. This was Sunday, April 17.

10 Buck Williams: Buckner Davis Williams (1833–1884), acting quartermaster of the 30th Regiment.

11 Dr. Cheek: "Dr. Benjamin A. Cheek, after service as a surgeon in the Confederate service, came to Warrenton to practice in 1867 and 1868. . . . The son of John Cheek of the county." Lizzie Wilson Montgomery, *Sketches of old Warrenton, North Carolina: Traditions and Reminiscences of the Town and People Who Made It* (Raleigh, Edwards & Broughton printing company, 1924).

12 not free: The sole reference to slaves or slavery in the memoir.

13 Hilliardston: In northwest Nash County.

14 that evening: Tuesday, April 18. The long walk home took seven days, finally bringing to an end three and a half years of marching.

15 In his last paragraph, JWB addresses the possibility of skepticism or disbelief in the minds of readers. He assures them that his experiences are seared in his mind and that his memory is sound. In his last, provocative sentence, he describes his storytelling as a kind of new, just-completed journey, filled with unexpected discoveries — some of which he decides to keep to himself.

10.

AFTER THE WAR

John Wesley Bone writes simply that he "reached my home that evening and found all well." Over three and a half years, he had traveled an estimated 3,996 miles: 1,201 on foot, 2,654 by train, and 141 by wagon, ambulance, boat, or on stretchers.[1] He saved the bullet that pierced his chest at Spotsylvania and his folding spoon and fork — both still in the family's possession. He was twenty-three years old, and set about earning a living as a farmer in the community of Oak Level, about ten miles from the town of Rocky Mount.[2]

In 1866, he acquired some practical items from the estate sale of his grandfather Nelson Bone. The most expensive item was a pair of cart wheels for six dollars. He bought practical farm tools: axes ($1.05), a shuck basket (20 cents), weed hoes (a nickel). A saddle ($2) and a horse brush (fifteen cents) imply that John Wesley owned a horse. A chest ($2.70) and six chairs ($2.75) were essentials for setting up a home, as were crockery, buckets, a flour barrel, and pots. The young veteran who had suffered so terribly for lack of shoes in wartime bought one personal item from the estate: a shoe brush, for fifteen cents. So, when he married Zillah Pridgen in 1868, his shoes were polished and the couple had a few essentials with which to set up housekeeping.

John Wesley Bone in 1898 with his wife, Zillah; son
Robert; and daughter Martha Ann, known as Pattie.
(Family collection)

Zillah and John Wesley had three children, Josiah May
(b. 1872), Robert Ernest (b. 1875), and Martha Ann (b. 1880). They
had six grandchildren and nine great-grandchildren. In an undated
photograph of the couple, John Wesley looks dashing in a dark
suit, starched white shirt, and white bow tie. A photograph from
1898 shows John Wesley and Zillah in their Sunday-best clothes,
seated in rocking chairs outside their home. Their son Robert and
daughter, Martha Ann, stand beside them.

His brothers all married, Henry in 1871, Josiah in 1886, and
Tinah in 1885. Among them they had a dozen children. All but
Henry lived out their lives near the family homestead. At one time
Tinah, Josiah, and John Wesley operated a cotton gin. Their father,
David, fell into debt and had to sell off his property. At the time of
his death he owned nothing except personal effects.

In 1896, John Wesley was appointed chairman of a seven-man group of trustees of Oak Level Academy, the first nine-month school in that community. They resolved to charge tuition for students, supplement the school payroll, and serve as arbitrators of disputes. Men in the Oak Level community contributed materials and labor to build the one-room school. The school building was expanded and had three teachers by the turn of the century. John Wesley's brothers Josiah and Tinah were also trustees.

Oak Level Baptist Church was organized in 1879. John Wesley served for many years as a deacon and at the time of his death was an honorary deacon. The congregation, numbering about sixty, posed in 1907 for a photograph in front of the wooden church building. Zillah and John Wesley are in the picture, along with their son Josiah and his wife, Mamie; son Robert; daughter, Martha Ann; and grandsons Walter Bone and James Daughtridge.

Although he lived a farmer's life and must have worked as hard as possible, John Wesley suffered physical effects of the war. North Carolina enacted a pension law in 1885 for Confederate veterans and their widows, and in 1901 expanded the law to include more beneficiaries. John Wesley applied for a pension on June 17, 1901. He stated the nature of the wound he suffered at Spotsylvania and concluded that its residual effects "render the body at this time in a weak and nervous condition when the body is exposed to much exercise, jolted or strained, [and] render it unfit for manual labor." A local board certified that he had no other government aid or income and did not own property with an assessed value for taxation to the amount of $500. He received the pension, amount unknown. (According to a granddaughter, he used some of his pension money to buy her parents an etched-glass cream and sugar set, still owned by the family.) However, even though he said he was "unfit for manual labor," it's clear that he was not a complete invalid. His 1936 obituary reports that he enjoyed riding horses until shortly before his death.

There is no evidence that John Wesley Bone was disabled

emotionally by his wartime experiences. He did not keep them
bottled up inside, as many veterans do — grandchildren remembered his dramatic war stories. He seems to have had the benefit of
a cheerful, positive temperament, as well as a lifelong trust that the
"Supreme Power" with beneficent purposes had charge of human
events.[3]

BESIDES HIS WAR MEMOIR, John Wesley wrote a brief history of
the Bone family in 1918. In his modest way he notes that the text
"may not be in proper form." In that family history John Wesley
writes of his grandfather Nelson Bone, "He accumulated a good
living, raised several slaves and gave his children a home." He does
not say that Nelson "owned" slaves but that he "raised" them,
perhaps making the point that in his family slaves were treated
respectfully and minimizing the fact that they were property.

The United Confederate Veterans was organized in 1889 in
New Orleans "to serve as a benevolent, historical, social and literary
association." At its height, the UCV had 160,000 members in 1,885
local chapters. John Wesley attended some of the UCV reunions.
He had a uniform made to wear to these gatherings, of blue-gray
wool with brass buttons stamped with the Confederate flag, the
letters "U.C.V.," and the dates 1861–1865. His son Josiah sometimes
accompanied him on the train when he went to Raleigh or Richmond for UCV reunions.

Confederate Veteran magazine published articles by veterans,
promoted reunions, and fostered research into the Confederate
cause. John Wesley subscribed, writing with his renewal in 1932, "I
am now in my ninetieth year, partly deaf and blind; almost the last
of the Confederate soldiers of Nash County; but I expect to take
the *Veteran* as long as I live, if I can."

In October 1925, "having a desire to visit these memorable places where I faced death and destruction many times," John Wesley traveled to Virginia to see certain battlefields again. Later, he wrote an article for the local newspaper, reprinted in 1926 in the *Confederate Veteran*. At Hamilton's Crossing, near Fredericksburg, he recalled, "I came so near being killed by a bomb." At Chancellorsville he "viewed the fields in which we crossed in taking the battery, where it seemed that we would all be killed." At Spotsylvania he "located about the very place where I lay, but the tree was gone and the house that then stood there had been burned." This article (reprinted below as "Postscript: Return to the Battlefields") supplied a few details of the fateful charge at the Bloody Angle not mentioned in *Record of a Soldier in the Late War:* that the men were ordered to "use our bayonets" before the charge ("every soldier knew what that meant"), and that an officer who had seen John Wesley fall reported him dead.

John Wesley Bone died of pneumonia on April 7, 1936, age ninety-three. A youth in the age of Lee, Grant, and Lincoln, he had lived into the age of Franklin Roosevelt. He was the last Confederate veteran in Nash County, having outlived by a few months George Washington Joyner, who enlisted with him in 1861. "At funeral services for John Wesley Bone this afternoon, Nash County citizens will pay tribute to the last of its Civil War heroes," read the notice in the *Nashville Graphic* on April 9. In his community, even after the country had gone through other great wars, those who had served in the "War Between the States" were revered. John Wesley and his wife, Zillah, who died in 1913, are buried in a family plot on land where his grandfather settled, which remains in the Bone family.

Although never edited and published before now, *Record of a Soldier in the Late War* has sometimes shown up in unexpected places. In the spring of 1992, our family vacationed in Virginia with the objective of visiting battle sites where John Wesley Bone had seen action. Three generations of Bones were on the journey, along with David Mehegan: Eloise Bone Faison, John Wesley's grand-daughter, who remembered Grandpa Bone and his war stories; Julianne Bone Mehegan, John Wesley's great-granddaughter; and her son Owen Bone Mehegan, twelve.

Armed with a copy of *Record of a Soldier in the Late War,* we began in Fredericksburg. There the National Park Service rangers brought out maps of the battle, showing the positions of the North Carolina 30th Regiment, confirming the commanders and actions recorded by John Wesley, who fought here December 11–13, 1862, near Hamilton's Crossing. We studied the maps and located his position before driving out to see the landscape.

We moved on to Chancellorsville, where John Wesley saw action with Stonewall Jackson April 30 – May 6, 1863, in one of the South's greatest victories. At the Battle of Chancellorsville, Jackson made a flank move to outwit General Hooker and push back the Union troops. Driving through dense, silent forests along Jackson's route, we read John Wesley's description of the "thick wilderness undergrowth" through which they marched.

At Spotsylvania Court House, where John Wesley was wounded in May 1864, we walked over the rolling landscape of mixed fields and woods, and stood at the foundation of the McCoull house, which he described as near where he lay on the battlefield.

At Appomattox Court House, we looked forward to comparing his account of the Confederate surrender with the preserved and restored site. The National Park Visitor Center was running a film program, *Honor Answers Honor,* which used texts from Union and Confederate soldiers' accounts, read by actors. As the program progressed, we were startled to hear a familiar passage: "I suppose that most of us on both sides took the quietest night rest that we had in many, for we were not dreading and watching for each other, for the lion and the lamb had now laid down together" — the words of John Wesley Bone. Two other sections of the program matched John Wesley's account word for word.

After returning home, we tracked down the source of the material used at Appomattox. The program was developed by the National Park Service in 1976. The script used material from several state archives, including those of North Carolina. Some of the Confederate material was taken from *Record of a Soldier in the Late War*. Before this discovery, John Wesley's family had no idea that his memoir was known to Civil War historians.

Thus we learned that John Wesley Bone's "plain outline" was indeed "worthy of a place on the record." We hope that in this edition, it will at last reach the wider audience it deserves.

Notes

1 JWB's travels were calculated by his great-great-grandson Jeff M. Mehegan. For a detailed breakdown of distances and modes of travel, see Appendix: A Soldier's Travels.

2 Although he found "all well" in that everyone was alive and home and property were intact, the economy of the South was a wreck and the financial system in chaos. In addition to mountains of paper money printed by the Richmond government, the North Carolina treasury had issued twenty-five different types of notes, worth little even before the Confederacy collapsed and worthless afterward. U.S. Legal Tender Notes — successor to the temporary greenbacks issued in the early years of the war — only gradually became widely available in the South. Inflation had exploded: the price of wheat had risen 1,600 percent by war's end and flour almost 2,800 percent. It would take time to follow General Lee's advice to "try to rebuild our lost fortunes," and for young survivors like JWB throughout the South, there was nothing to do but get started.

3 In the emotional as much as the physical stresses of war, youth was in his favor. Eric T. Dean writes, "The experience of World War II revealed that the age group which experienced the fewest problems were those aged eighteen to twenty-five; with age, there was a sharp rise in psychoneurosis, for instance from 6 per thousand in eighteen- and nineteen-year-olds to 45 per thousand in thirty-six- and thirty-seven-year olds" (Dean, 37).

11.

POSTSCRIPT:
RETURN TO THE BATTLEFIELDS

Sixty years after the end of the war, John Wesley returned to several of the battlefields on which he had fought. He wrote about this visit, apparently his last written words on the war. Two versions of this text survive: the first written for the December 3, 1925, issue of the *Nashville Graphic,* John Wesley's local weekly newspaper, the second a reprint in a 1926 issue of the *Confederate Veteran* magazine. A tattered original copy of the *Graphic* version is our text, as well as a very poor microfilm copy of it preserved in the Braswell Memorial Library in Rocky Mount, North Carolina. Where those copies are torn, missing sections, or illegible, the *Confederate Veteran* version was used.

REMINISCENCES FROM PEN OF NASH COUNTY VETERAN
*Pays Visit to Old Battlegrounds and Envisions
Thrilling Experiences Through Which He Passed*

By John W. Bone, Nashville, N.C.

I was a soldier in the Civil War from '61 to '65 and followed Lee and Jackson through many of the battles fought by the army of Northern Virginia, and surrendered with Lee at Appomattox.

For some time I had the desire to visit these memorable old places where I faced death and destruction many times and this desire would bring to my mind many a scene of the past.

So sometime in the past October I made my way to Fredericksburg, Va., where the awful battle was fought December 13th, 1862. The Federal army was commanded by Gen. Burnside who put his forces across the Rappahannock river on pontoons, and attacked Lee's army on the south side.

I viewed the place that was called Hamilton's Crossing, where D. H. Hill's division fought, to which I belonged, and where I came so near being killed by a bomb, which just missed me, wounding a man just in my rear, from which he died. I also viewed Marye's Heights, where we slaughtered the enemy in great numbers. After the 13th there being no other engagement, only the sharpshooters and cannonaders being actively employed, we remained in the line of battle for about three days. On the night of the third day the Federal army withdrew across the river, leaving a large number of dead and prisoners. Jackson's corps had just come over from the valley and were poorly shod and clothed, for we had not received much of either since the previous August, when we left Richmond for the Maryland campaign. While we remained in position it rained and froze, turning awfully cold. We suffered terribly, the army being in the worst shape at that time than perhaps it ever was during the whole four years.

I now visited the old historical town located on the banks of the Rappahannock river. It is now a beautiful town with a large number of inhabitants. I went down on the river banks where along in the cold winter of '63 I stayed for one week on picket duty and had to stand four hours at night (two at a time) and walk my post from end to end along a narrow track with the snow about three feet deep and the cold wind blowing across the river from Stafford Heights and when relieved at the end of two hours, a very poor shelter to remain under and but little fire.

I then visited the cemetery where a large number of Confederate soldier were buried. It was nicely kept. I then passed the Federal cemetery, where I was told that upward of 15,000 soldiers were buried, having been taken from the different fields of battle around Fredericksburg. It was a fine looking place, but I did not take time to visit it as it was getting late.

I now took what was once the plank road leading from Fredericksburg to Orange Court House, a distance of about forty miles, but now a smooth dirt road. On the road about five miles from the town I came to Salem Church. I remembered that Gen. Joe Hooker had been put in command of the Grand Army of the Potomac and had 150,000 men at his command, while Gen. Lee with the army of Northern Virginia on the south side of the river had 50,000 Confederate soldiers, a part of this army being sent to other places. About the last days of April '63 Gen. Hooker commenced putting his army across the Rappahannock river at three places, on his march to Richmond, namely: at Fredericksburg up near Salem church and the large body up at Chancellorsville about twelve miles above Fredericksburg. Jackson's corps were camping near and below the town. The command that I belonged to, the 30th North Carolina regiment, was at that time on picket duty on the river just below the town. There was a call for a corps of sharpshooters to meet the enemy. I was one, and we met them near the Cedar Road there through the day and remained there through the night.

The next morning Jackson was ordered to go in the direction of Chancellorsville, which he did, this being May 1. We remained on the line for some time, but were relieved after a while and followed our commander, overtaking the corps before they struck the enemy above Salem Church, and we fought until night, then lay in line through the night, slumbering on our muskets, if slumber we did. We were near the place where Lee and Jackson were together for the last time (there is a marker at the place).

The next morning, May 2, we were expecting to be ordered forward, but to our surprise we were ordered to the rear, this being the time when Jackson started his great and successful last flank movement. We marched in quick and double-quick time and for several hours, and in the evening struck the enemy in the rear, fighting until dark. We had reached the plank road and my command (Ramseur's Brigade) was on the east side. We were ordered to take off the most of our baggage and be ready to make a night attack. Jackson was investigating the front as he returned, when he and his staff were mistaken for the enemy and fired upon by our own men, wounding [him] and causing his death. We were about two hundred yards below the road. That stopped the attack for the night. The next morning we were ordered forward in support of another line. During the night the enemy had made temporary breastworks and cut down the growth in front of the line before we reached the works, taking them; but the enemy's line of support reached them before we did and took them back, we being in about thirty yards at the time making our way through the logs and brush. At this point the line in our front commenced falling back and, to prevent confusion, we were ordered to lie down until the men passed us, when we were ordered forward and took the works. At this time the enemy had a cross fire on us from our right and a battery in our front near Chancellor's house, but we turned our fire to the right and soon drove the enemy back. We were then ordered to charge the artillery in front of us, which was killing and wounding us rapidly, it being about half a mile from us in the open field. We charged and took it.

This just about ended the battle up here except the skirmishing and cannonading. We did not realize our condition until it was all over, and it was well that we did not, for we then realized that of seventy men we had started with in the morning, half were killed or wounded. On the morning of May 3, before we started, there were with us two brothers from the same county as myself (Nash), good boys and good soldiers. The younger went to the older and told him to take his rations and pocketbook, for he would be killed that day — and when the battle was over he was one among the dead.

Going back to Salem Church, which now has many markers near it in honor of some of the Federal regiments that fought and suffered near there, while Jackson's men were driving back the Federals at Fredericksburg and Salem Church, there was great slaughter of them at the river. So "Fighting" Joe soon passed back across the river with his good army, with the exception of those he had to leave on the other side. Going down the dirt road, I saw the old sunken road that I had traveled in those days and which leads down to Hamilton's Crossing. I then came to the Chancellor house, a large, two-story brick building and basement, showing signs of war, with many pieces of shells lying around it. Passing to the rear of the enclosure, I saw where there was a heavy forest at that time, but which was burned off. I had been sent with others to stop the fire and remove the wounded. I viewed the fields in which we crossed in taking the battery, where it seemed that we would all be killed. Continuing down the road where we had remained until the enemy disappeared, I viewed the woods where I was put on the front sharpshooter's line one dark, rainy night, and I remembered how the whippoorwills would cry, their clear notes ringing near me — and how my thoughts went back to my boyhood days at home.

I went to the place where Jackson received his death wound near the old road. I was so near on that night that I heard the firing of the guns that wounded him. A handsome monument now stands at the place. The day being far spent, I made my way to Mr. Strickland's house, a few miles beyond Spotsylvania Courthouse, and near the National Highway, and spent the night in that hospitable home.

The next morning, in company with a gentleman and two ladies, we started for that part of the [Spotsylvania Court House] battlefield known as the Bloody Angle, a place that I have wanted to visit since I was there sixty-one years ago. On our way near the court house we came to a large Confederate cemetery, it being wired and with a big monument.[1] In it were the dead from the battlefields Chancellorsville and Spotsylvania had been taken from and buried there. We now came to the edge of the Wilderness, where stood a large monument erected to some Federal General who was killed at the battle of the Wilderness, May 1864.[2]

We came to an old road that we had camped on the 8th day of May, 1864, a very warm day, so hot that many men fainted and fell by the wayside. We had threatened General Grant at the Wilderness and he was now moving his army down to Spotsylvania. It was on the 8th day and we had been fighting since the 5th day. We met his army that evening and had a right heavy engagement, threw up breastworks and made ready for a retreat, this being Sunday. We remained in our works for three days, the sharpshooters firing on our front day and night and engagements on our right and left every day, but we were not engaged until the 12th of that May; about a quarter of a mile to our right was the angle our line made in order to get the elevation of the land for the advantage of the artillery. We held our lines well. The enemy tried to see if they could get that angle so they could move their artillery there and turn up and down our lines, and so they did.[3] So after taking it, to let the reader understand better about the capture of the angle, I will relate the experience that one who was on the enemy's side and in the charge said on the morning of the 12th. Before day they formed seven lines of men behind each other and did not let them have loaded guns and gave them so much whiskey as was necessary and told them to take the angle, and so they did. We had one line, but our men stood to them hand to hand and until it was no use to try any longer and fell back or surrendered.

The enemy had completed his object, and mounted the artillery and turned it up and down our lines. Something had to be done and that quickly. General Ramseur believed in obeying orders and did not mind fighting when it was needed. He was ordered to take his North Carolina Brigade and get the angle back. We were formed in front of a low place and ordered to use our bayonets.[4]

Every soldier knew what that meant. The General said: "Colonel, we have got to take the works, and we can do it." We were now in about three hundred yards of the angle, and they crossed fire on us, men being killed and wounded and it was awful, but we stood firm awaiting orders. We had passed through so much for the eight days that fear had almost left us, but we feared wounds or death to some extent. The command was now given to go forward. We assembled on a small place and passed the sharpshooters, the balls and shells coming thick! We were then ordered to charge. We took a trot and gave the rebel yell and went to the angle and had it hand to hand for a while. Finally, the enemy seeing our determination, gave back. Both sides remained and held their line, the lines being near together. There was a regular fire kept up all day and all night. A steady round of cannonading and musketry was kept up for about twenty hours. About day on the morning of the 13th the Confederates fell back and had a little rest, which was badly needed. There were more men killed at that place during the battle than in any one day during the Civil War.[5]

I was told by those that buried the dead that many were found lying on each other in places. There were markers erected in honor of some of the Federal soldiers. I came to a place where a tree fifteen inches in diameter was cut down by bullets. The stump had been taken up and put in the museum in Washington city. The place was marked by a light wood post. A man now living on the hill said that he was a boy living there and had to leave home and on returning found three N. Carolina soldiers dead under the tree.

I will now give a sad but fortunate experience of mine in this battle. I was in the charge and just before reaching the angle was shot through the body and hit by a ball which I now have. It went through me and lodged in a pack that I carried. I knew that I was hit bad, but did not know how bad. My officer seeing me go down thought that I was killed and reported me dead, but I was not dead and soon began to try to get out. I was bleeding very freely, and the shells and balls were coming thick, but I began trying to get to the rear. I could go only a short way at a time, and was hit by two more balls, but I managed to get to the top of the hill and behind a small tree in the open field. At that time, I had lost so much blood and was so weak I could not go farther. I was hoping that the battle would end and I would be taken out, but they did not stop until about day the next morning, when our men fell back. I was weak, wet, cold, thirsty, and sleepy, but was not aware of my condition until I was aroused by the fire of a gun near me. I glanced to my rear and saw a line of sharpshooters advancing. I then saw that I was between both lines and on "No-Man's-Land," for neither could come to me without being killed.[6] I would have then given anything if I could have been with my friends. I remained in this condition for two more days and nights, hoping that there would be some change and on the last evening hearing the enemy moving their artillery and firing on our men I decided that they would advance the next morning. Things looked very serious to me for without some change that would be my last resting place. Oh! the three days and nights that I spent there seemed like a life time! And seeing no relief in sight I lifted my heart, mind, and soul to the Supreme Power that rules over all, asking help me get away from there. The moon shone until nearly day, and when it was gone from sight I made an effort to get away, and by moving by little I got near our line and was helped.

It is a desolate place now, a few people live around, the fields have grown in bushes to a great extent. I located about the very place I lay, the tree being gone, the house that then stood has been burned down. Notwithstanding all this I was so thankful to the Supreme Power that I was living, after sixty-one years was able to come back and realize something that I never had before. I have tried to live a consecrated life, but as I stood there and viewed the place, I thought [about the] wretched man that I am, escaping death here and helping to fight other battles, surrendering at Appomattox. I am now in my eighty-fourth year [and] have done so little [to attend to what is] spiritual of man.[7]

Notes

1 wired: surrounded by a wire fence.

2 Federal General: The monument at Spotsylvania is to Major General John Sedgwick, the most senior Union officer to die in battle. He was killed May 9, 1864, at long range by a Confederate sharpshooter.

3 that angle: That is, the Mule Shoe salient, of which the Bloody Angle was a small section.

4 in front of a low place: Possibly *in* a low place.
use our bayonets: Bayonets are not mentioned in the 1904 memoir.

5 more men: The day of greatest loss of life in the war was September 17, 1962, at the Battle of Antietam, when more than 22,000 were killed or wounded.

6 No-Man's-Land: An ancient term for disputed territory. Its use for a battlefield area between the lines dates mostly from the British army in World War I.

7 The last paragraph of the *Confederate Veteran* version was edited to remove the religious content. It ends, "I was able to come back and realize something that I never had before. After escaping death and helping to fight other battles, then surrendering at Appomattox, I have been spared into my eighty-fourth year." This makes no sense; he did not just then realize his age. Enough of the tattered *Graphic* version survives — a few conjectural words are added in brackets here — to make his meaning clear. He is feeling a pang of conscience as he stands in old age at this quiet and "desolate place" of long-ago slaughter. Looking back over his life, he suspects that he has fallen short of his duty as a Christian in return for the gift of survival. It is as if he believes that God must have allowed him to live for a discernible purpose, to fulfill some spiritual good work. Otherwise, that so many good men should have died, while he lived, would have no meaning. In addition to physical scars, here is a spiritual wound that never fully healed.

Appendix

A SOLDIER'S TRAVELS

This estimate of the wartime movements of John Wesley Bone was prepared by his great-great-grandson Jeff Mehegan, a U.S. Army veteran and transportation specialist. All distances are in miles. Estimates are based on the text, with consultation of road maps, historical railroad maps, and various online historical resources and transportation software.

By foot:	1,201
By train:	2,654
By wagon or ambulance:	109
By boat:	32
Total miles:	**3,996**

1861	
September	
Nashville to Raleigh via Spring Hope, Zebulon, Wendell, and Knightdale	50 by train
October–December	
Raleigh to Wilmington via Goldsboro, Mt. Olive, Warsaw, Wallace, Burgaw	137 by train
1862	
January–February	
Wilmington to Fort Caswell, Smithville/Southport	22 by boat, 30 on foot
Fort Caswell to Fort Wyatt	10 by boat
Fort Wyatt to Wilmington	23 by "four mule wagon"
Fort Wyatt to home on furlough	124 by train via Wilmington
Home to Wilmington	112 by train
March	
Wilmington to home on 15-day furlough	112 by train
Home to Wilmington	112 by train
April–May	
Wilmington to Jacksonville, Onslow County, "a distance of nearly one hundred miles"	actually 88 on foot
Jacksonville to Wrightsville Sound	95 on foot
Wrightsville to Wilmington	9 on foot

June	
Wilmington to Capitol Square, Richmond	258 by train
June 26–30	
Seven Days' Battles, Gaines's Mill, Malvern Hill	49 on foot, plus 8 by wagon
August	
Richmond to Culpeper	82 on foot
Culpeper to Manassas via Orange and Alexandria Railroad tracks	40 on foot
September	
Manassas to Sharpsburg, halted at Leesburg for lack of shoes	29 on foot
October–November	
Leesburg to Winchester	37 on foot
December	
Picket duty and "tearing up railroads" between Winchester and Harpers Ferry	18 on foot
1863	
January–March	
Winchester to Fredericksburg	80 on foot
Fredericksburg picket duty, "marched out and went some distance up the river"	30 on foot
May	
Chancellorsville	19 on foot

June	
Fredericksburg, Culpeper, Brandy Station	42 on foot
June 12	
To Gordonsville Hospital,	7 by ambulance, 29 by train
July	
Gordonsville to home on furlough via Richmond, Danville, Greensboro, Raleigh	412 by train
August–September	
Home to Gordonsville	412 by train
October–November	
Gordonsville to Fredericksburg	46 by train
Fredericksburg to Kelly's Ford and movements around area	42 on foot
Wilderness to Orange	28 by ambulance
December–February	
Orange to Charlottesville	28 by train
1864	
March–April	
Charlottesville to Gordonsville	20 by train
"Sent to command about ten miles south of Orange"	26 on foot
Various duties, picket duty	24 on foot
May 5	
Wilderness area	12 on foot
May 9–13	
Wilderness to Spotsylvania Court House	8 on foot

June	
Field hospital near Spotsylvania to Orange	43 by ambulance
Orange to Gordonsville Hospital	9 by train
July 16–17	
Gordonsville to home on furlough	412 by train
October	
Home to Richmond via Danville	125 by train
Richmond to Staunton	104 by train
Staunton to Cedar Creek	75 on foot
Battle of Cedar Creek	5 on foot
Cedar Creek to New Market camp	34 on foot
November–December	
New Market to Staunton	43 on foot
Staunton to Petersburg	152 by train
1865	
January–March	
Camp at Petersburg, Appomattox River guard duty, Petersburg area fighting	14 on foot
Retreat from Petersburg to Amelia Court House	43 on foot
Amelia Court House to High Bridge, near Farmville	21 on foot
High Bridge to Farmville	5 on foot

March	
Moving skirmishes west from Farmville	6 on foot
April 9–12	
Farmville area to Appomattox Court House	28 on foot. War ends.
April 13–17	
Appomattox Court House to home via Marysville, Roanoke River at Taylor's Ferry, Warrenton, Hilliardston	148 on foot

Acknowledgments

W e are indebted to members of the Bone family: Eloise Bone Faison, Eunice Bone, and Kenneth Bone, for their efforts to preserve artifacts and knowledge of John Wesley Bone, and for essential remembered details of his unwritten recollections. We are indebted as well to Ella Margaret Bone Cron and Frederick Holmes Cron, for their extensive research into the Bone family and organization of the material in book form. Our son, Jeff Mehegan, researched the distance traveled by his great-great-grandfather over the course of the war, and compiled the excellent and revealing appendix, "A Soldier's Travels."

Several Civil War historians and researchers gave important advice or information, including Frank A. O'Reilly and Donald Pfanz at the Fredericksburg and Spotsylvania National Military Park, and Robert E. L. (Bobby) Krick of the Chimborazo Medical Museum in the Richmond National Battlefield Park. Professor Terry L. Jones of Louisiana State University at Monroe contributed key details about the French-speaking Confederates at Spotsylvania Court House. William M. Fowler Jr., distinguished professor of history at Northeastern University, kindly provided support and suggestions.

Teresa Roane, archivist of the United Daughters of the Confederacy and former library manager at the Museum of the Confederacy in Richmond, was helpful in unearthing JWB's service and hospital records. Cartographer Hal Jespersen granted permission to use his excellent battlefield maps. We are thankful to Dr. Peter Moyer, professor emeritus in emergency medicine at Boston University School of Medicine, for his analysis of John Wesley Bone's wound at Spotsylvania Court House. We are especially grateful to Jack Betts, former writer and associate editor of the Charlotte *Observer*, for use of the photograph of his great-grandfather, Rev. A.D. Betts.

Works Cited

Alexander, Edward Porter. *Fighting for the Confederacy: The Personal Recollections of General Edward Porter Alexander.* Gary W. Gallagher, ed. Chapel Hill: University of North Carolina Press, 1989.

Barton, Michael, and Larry M. Logue. *The Civil War Soldier: A Historical Reader.* New York: New York University Press, 2002.

Betts, A. D., W. A. Betts, ed. *Experience of a Confederate Chaplain, 1861–1864.* Whitefish, Mont.: Kessinger Publishing, 2010. Originally published 1906.

Black, Robert C. III. *The Railroads of the Confederacy.* Chapel Hill: University of North Carolina Press, 1998.

Calcutt, Rebecca Barbour. *Richmond's Wartime Hospitals.* Gretna, La.: Pelican Publishing Co, 2005.

Clark, Walter, ed. *Histories of the Several Regiments and Battalions from North Carolina in the Great War 1861–'65.* 5 vols. Raleigh, N.C.: E. M. Uzzell, 1901.

Cron, Frederick Holmes. *The Bone Family: Distant Voices from the Water's Edge.* Wyandotte, Okla.: The Gregath Publishing Co., 1999.

Cunningham, H. H. *Doctors in Gray: The Confederate Medical Service,* 2nd ed. Baton Rouge: Louisiana State University Press, 1960.

Dean, Eric T. *Shook over Hell: Post-Traumatic Stress, Vietnam, and the Civil War.* Cambridge: Harvard University Press, 1999.

Dollar, Kent T. "'Strangers in a Strange Land': Christian Soldiers in the Early Months of the Civil War," *The View from the Ground: Experiences of Civil War Soldiers.* Aaron Sheehan-Dean, ed. Lexington: University Press of Kentucky, 2007.

Donald, David Herbert. "The Confederate as a Fighting Man." *Journal of Southern History* 25, May 1959.

Faust, Drew Gilpin. "Christian Soldiers: The Meaning of Revivalism in the Confederate Army." *Journal of Southern History* 53, no. 1, February 1987.

___. *This Republic of Suffering: Death and the American Civil War.* New York: Alfred A. Knopf, 2008.

Fletcher, William A. *Rebel Private, Front and Rear: Memoirs of a Confederate Soldier.* New York: E. P. Dutton, 1995; originally published 1908.

Frank, Lisa Tendrich. *Women in the American Civil War, Volume 1.* Santa Barbara: ABC-CLIO Inc., 2008.

Freeman, Douglas Southall. *Lee: An Abridgement by Richard Harwell.* New York: Scribners, 1991.

Gugliotta, Guy. "New Estimate Raises Civil War Death Toll." *New York: New York Times,* April 3, 2012.

Glatthaar, Joseph T. *Soldiering in the Army of Northern Virginia: A Statistical Portrait of the Troops Who Served under Robert E. Lee.* Chapel Hill: University of North Carolina Press, 2011.

Grant, Ulysses S. *Personal Memoirs of U .S. Grant, Volume 2.* New York: Charles Webster and Co., 1886.

Imboden, John D. "The Confederate Retreat from Gettysburg," *Battles and Leaders of the Civil War,* Vol. 3. New York: Castle Books, 1956.

Jones, Terry L. *The American Civil War.* New York: McGraw-Hill, 2008.

___. *Lee's Tigers: The Louisiana Infantry in the Army of Northern Virginia.* Baton Rouge: Louisiana State University Press, 2002.

Lonn, Ella. *Desertion during the Civil War.* Lincoln: University of Nebraska Press, 1998; originally published 1928.

McCarthy, Carlton. *Detailed Minutiae of Soldier Life in the Army of Northern Virginia, 1861–1865.* Richmond: C. McCarthy, 1882.

Medicine of the Civil War. Rockville, Md: National Library of Medicine, 1973.

Montgomery, Lizzie Wilson. *Sketches of Old Warrenton, North Carolina: Traditions and Reminiscences of the Town and People Who Made It.* Raleigh: Edwards & Broughton printing company, 1924.

Pember, Phoebe Yates. *A Southern Woman's Story.* Whitefish, Mont.: Kessinger Publishing, 2010.

Rutkow, Ira M. *Bleeding Blue and Gray: Civil War Surgery and the Evolution of American Medicine.* New York: Random House, 2005.

Sartin, J.S. "Infectious Diseases during the Civil War: The Triumph of the 'Third Army.'" Arlington, Va.: *Clinical Infectious Diseases,* April 1993.

Sheehan-Dean, Aaron. *The View from the Ground: Experiences of Civil War Soldiers.* Lexington: University Press of Kentucky, 2007.

Taylor, Michael W. *To Drive the Enemy from Southern Soil: The Letters of Col. Francis Marion Parker and the History of the 30th Regiment North Carolina Troops.* Dayton, Ohio: Morningside House, 1998.

Tucker, Spencer C. *Brigadier General John D. Imboden: Confederate Commander in the Shenandoah.* Lexington: University Press of Kentucky, 2002.

Waddell, Joseph A. *Annals of Augusta County Virginia: From 1726 to 1871.* Staunton, Va.: C. Russell Caldwell, 1902.

Waitt, Robert W. Jr. *Confederate Military Hospitals in Richmond.* Richmond: Official Publication No. 22, Richmond Civil War Centennial Committee, 1964.

Weitz, Mark A. *More Damning than Slaughter: Desertion in the Confederate Army.* Lincoln: University of Nebraska Press, 2005.

Welch, Jack D. *Two Confederate Hospitals and Their Patients: Atlanta to Opelika.* Macon: Mercer University Press, 2005.

Wiley, Bell Irvin. *The Life of Johnny Reb: The Common Soldier of the Confederacy.* Baton Rouge: Louisiana State University Press, 1978.

CPSIA information can be obtained at www.ICGtesting.com
Printed in the USA
LVOW06s0209121214

418486LV00003B/214/P